BARCELONA

COMPLETE GUIDE
TO THE CITY

THE MONUMENTS, HISTORY AND FUTURE
OF THE 'CAPITAL OF THE MEDITERRANEAN'

BONECHI

Publication created and designed by *Casa Editrice Bonechi*
Editorial management: *Giovanna Magi*
Graphic design, layout, make up and cover: *Sonia Gottardo*
Text: *Giovanna Magi, Patrizia Chirichigno* and *Patrizia Fabbri*
Translation: *Studio Comunicare, Florence; Eve Leckey*
Drawings: *Stefano Benini*

© Copyright by Casa Editrice Bonechi,via Cairoli 18/b , Firenze - Italia
Tel +39 055 576841 - Fax +39 055 5000766

E-mail: bonechi@bonechi.it – www.bonechi.com

Printed in Italy by *Centro Stampa Editoriale Bonechi*.

The majority of the photographs are property of the *Casa Editrice Bonechi* Archives.
They were taken by
*Marco Bonechi, Serena De Leonardis, Andrea Fantauzzo, Paolo Giambone,
Andrea Pistolesi, Alessandro Saragosa.*

Other photographs were provided by
Museu Barbier-Mueller/Art Precolombí: pages 28-29. *Andrea Ghisotti:*
page 60 below. *Sonia Gottardo:* pages 82 above, 84 below. *Andrea Pistolesi:*
pages 10-11, 34 above, 35 below, 36 above right, 37, 38 below, 140.
Pepo Segura - Fundació Mies van der Rohe/Barcelona: pages 126, 127 above
and below left.

Photographs on pages 126, 127 above and below left, courtesy of
Fundació Mies van der Rohe/Barcelona

Plan of metro, courtesy of *Transports Metropolitans de Barcelona.*

The publisher apologises for any omissions and is willing to make amends with
the formal recognition of the author of any photo subsequently identified.

ISBN 88-476-1290-X

* * *

INTRODUCTION

In its splendid site upstream from the mouth of the Llobregat, the capital of Catalonia is attractively framed by mount Montjuïc and Tibidabo, one of the peaks of the Sierra de Collserola The coast to the north of Barcelona, which stretches for kilometres, includes the well-known resorts of the Costa Brava, one of the most popular international tourist destinations. With over one and a half million inhabitants, Barcelona is the second most populous city in Spain and, as an important port and industrial pole, its image is that of a large metropolitan centre. The urban fabric of the city is both old and new at the same time, fascinating and picturesque, and these various aspects are evident in the geometric linearity of the urban blocks in the city centre with broad fast-flow traffic boulevards on either side, and in the entrancing Mediterranean jumble of the so-called Barri Gòtic, the ancient medieval heart of the city.

The Catalan capital is verdant and full of trees, parks and gardens; the squares and boulevards, magnificently shaded by decorative palms and tall trees, reflect the image of a great Mediterranean metropolis, blessed with a felicitous climate. To think of Barcelona only in terms of bull fights, flamenco and paella is to limit the image of the city to the most commonplace of tourist stereotypes. In reality the capital of Catalonia has a host of cultural and artistic aspects which range from an ancient linguistic tradition – the Catalan language is being used more and more, even on an official level as opposed to Castilian – to the surprising examples of ancient and modern Gothic art, including some of the most stupendous, breathtaking and fabulous creations of art nouveau. This city, an eclectic synthesis of architectural styles – Gothic, renaissance and neo-classical – was the experimental workshop of Antoni Gaudí, who left indelible examples of his surrealistic abstract art, and also inspired the pictorial genius of Picasso, who lived here in two specific periods, considered among the most productive of his fertile artistic career.

Life in Barcelona – which in the evening and at night-time becomes a lively celebration – the magical enchantment of the Ramblas, perennially crowded with towns-people and tourists, characterized by the stalls where flowers, birds and articles of all kinds are sold, the picturesque antique market and the fascinating flea market, large department stores, the marvelous Catalan food, the folklore of the Sardana – a regional folk dance – are all elements which the tourist will long remember after admiring the imposing monuments, the colours and lights of this extraordinary city. Having hosted the Olympic Games in 1992, today Barcelona is excellently endowed with reception and service infrastructures. Recently-built modern sports facilities, together with newly-renovated modern buildings, provided hospitality for this important international event which became a source of pride for Barcelona at the beginning of the last decade of the 20th century.

HISTORY

ORIGINS

Barcelona was first established as a trading centre by the Phoenicians and the Greeks. Various legends exist to explain how the city got its name of *Barcino*. According to one, the city was founded by Hercules, on one of his trips from Thebes, together with the survivors of the ninth vessel of the expedition. Another version takes the origin of the city back to the Carthaginians, who called it *Barcino* in honour of Hannibal's father, Amilcare Barca. Be that as it may, these and other legends are contradicted by the archaeological finds in the city which indicate that indigenous populations already lived at the foot of Montjuïc when the Roman expeditions decided to settle there.

THE ROMAN PERIOD

Around the end of the 1st century B.C. the Roman colony *Iulia Augusta Faventia Paterna Barcino* was founded near the slopes of Mount Taber. It was then provided with walls and laid out so that the roads would lead from the sea towards the mountains, and perpendicularly, from the river Besos to the river Llobregat.

THE BARBARIAN INVASIONS

Roman domination lasted six centuries until, with the decline of the Empire, the barbarian invasions began. In order to protect the city, the walls which surrounded the future city of Barcelona were reinforced around the 4th century. It was conquered by the Visigoths and the Vandals, and although Ataulf then transformed it into the temporary capital of the Visigothic realm, it lost none of its religious importance, for councils were held there both in 540 and 589.

THE ARABS AND THEIR DEFEAT

Later Spain became a theatre for the struggle between Christianity and Islam. The Arabs seized Barcelona in 716 and occupied it until 801 when the troops of Louis the Pious, son of Charlemagne, reconquered the city, transforming it into the *Hispanic March* of the Frankish empire. The Garraf massifs constituted the frontier between the Arab and the Christian worlds. Wilfred the Hairy (*Gulfred el Pilos*), a Catalan national hero, fought against the Arabs together with Charles the Bald. In reward for this courage the French king granted Barcelona independence.

THE MIDDLE AGES

In the Middle Ages, under the dominion of the counts of Barcelona, the city enjoyed a period of great splendour and incomparable development, and profitable trade relations were established with Genoa and Venice. After union with Provence, Ramón Berenguer IV (1131-1162) contracted marriage with an Aragonese princess, and a vast and stable realm came into being at the heart of the Iberian peninsula.

Barcelona was on the threshold of its golden age. James the Conqueror drove the Saracens from the Balearic Islands (from Majorca in 1235 and from Ibiza in 1238). Barcelona's rule stretched all the way to Sicily, to Corsica, Sardinia and even as far as Greece. At that time Barcelona was the first port in the Mediterranean and the most important city in Spain, a role which it held until the discovery of America. The construction of Barcelona's shipyards (*Drassanes* or *Atarazanas*), begun by James I, dates from this period (13th century). But a sequence of military and political events brought about a long period of crisis and instability starting in the 13th century.

URBAN DEVELOPMENT

Despite this, it was between the 4th and the 13th century that Barcelona consolidated the urban nucleus founded by the Romans and began an expansion which would determine the future of the city. From the point of view of town planning, the most characteristic features of this period are the appearance of suburbs, known as the *viles noves* (new towns) as well as improvements made to the city. At the end of the 13th century a new circle of walls was built, enclosing what today is the old centre, aimed at protecting the most active *viles noves* – those centres of population scattered in the surroundings, and the new suburbs concentrated around what is now Santa María del Mar. During these centuries Barcelona was characterized by its great public buildings such as the cathedral, the Palace of the Government (Palau de la Generalitat), the Port, Santa María del Pi, the Royal Palace (Palau del Rei), the Council of the Hundred (*Consell de Cent*), the Llotja.

FROM THE RENAISSANCE TO MODERN TIMES

The new maritime routes that opened up with the discovery of America meant a rapid decline in the fortunes of Barcelona and the centre of power in the peninsula shifted towards Madrid and the cities of the south. The city, under the jurisdiction of a Count, began a difficult period, more than once rebelling against the central government and the Bourbon dynasty of Spain.

THE 18TH CENTURY

The 18th century began with the surrender of the city, on September 11, 1714, to the Bourbon troops of Philip V. By a curious coincidence, September 11 is "*La diada*", the national holiday of Catalonia. The price of these revolts was high: the city lost its autonomy, the Courts (*Corts*), the Government (*Generalitat*) and the Council of the Hundred (*Consell de Cent*) were all suppressed and the Catalan language was outlawed. During the 18th century some of the key infrastructures of the city were destroyed. In the northern part more than a thousand buildings were razed to the ground to make room for the construction of a military fort and a new quarter for the fishermen's district was planned, now Barceloneta. Not until the reign of Charles III did Barcelona make a comeback. The port was reopened to trade with America and rapid new growth began again. In 1775, based on a project by Count Ricla, work began on *La Rambla*, the most famous and characteristic promenade of the city.

THE 19TH CENTURY

The expansion of the city towards the plain commenced in 1859 and the medieval walls which surrounded the city were razed to the ground. "*El Eixample*", which linked the city centre to surrounding villages, such as Gracia, Sants, Les Corts, now districts within the city, was the brainchild of the engineer Ildefonso Cerdá. Rationality and functionality lay at the basis of the plan which took into account the industrial nature of the city and its communications network. Unfortunately, as a result of speculation, it was never faithfully carried out. To the great joy of the people of Barcelona, the military fortress of La Ciutadella was destroyed to make way for a park with a museum dedicated to science. The old fortress thus became part of the general project for the expansion and reconstruction of the city, now well on its way to completion. In 1885 the mayor of the city, Rius i Taulet, made the space previously occupied by the hated fortress available for the city's first Universal Exhibition.

THE 20TH CENTURY

The *Pla Macià*, planned at the beginning of the 20th century, was an ambitious project for the urban renewal of the city, but was unfortunately interrupted by the Civil War. The mass arrival of immigrants resulted in a spectacular rise in the population and led to the deterioration and suburbanization of the glorious Barcelona of the 1931 Republic. When democracy was restored at the end of the 1970s, Barcelona undertook a series of urbanistic initiatives to recuperate the free spaces for public utility and recreational structures, to renovate districts and buildings and reorganize the city's communications system and thoroughfares, all of which had badly deteriorated, in an attempt to achieve a new territorial equilibrium. When Barcelona was proposed and then proclaimed host to the 1992 Olympic Games, the city seemed to recuperate its lost pride and image. Its damaged inner fabric has been renovated with the new metropolitan plan and the suburbs have been urbanized. Project Barcelona '92 provided a new impulse and a new objective for the reorganization, restoration and reconstruction processes of the city's urban fabric.

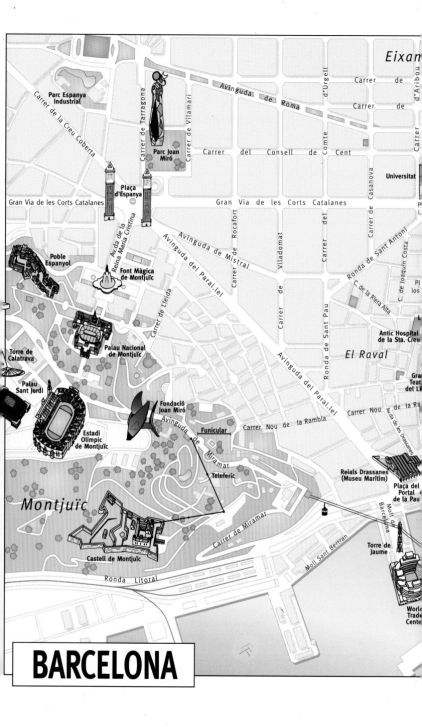

Eixample

Parc Espanya Industrial

Carrer de la Creu Coberta

Avinguda de Roma

Carrer de Tarragona

Carrer de Vilamarí

Carrer d'Urgell

Carrer de

Carrer de

Carrer d'Aribau

Parc Joan Miró

Carrer del Consell de Cent

Comte d'Urgell

Carrer de Casanova

Universitat

Plaça d'Espanya

Gran Via de les Corts Catalanes

Gran Via de les Corts Catalanes

Carrer de

Carrer de Rocafort

Carrer del

Carrer de Sant Antoni

Avda. de la Reina Maria Cristina

Avinguda de Mistral

Carrer de Viladomat

Ronda de Sant Antoni

C. de Joaquín Costa

Poble Espanyol

Avinguda del Paral.lel

Font Màgica de Montjuïc

Pl. los

Carrer de Lleida

Carrer de

Carrer de Sant Pau

C. de la Riera Alta

Torre de Calatrava

Palau Nacional de Montjuïc

Antic Hospital de la Sta. Creu

El Raval

Palau Sant Jordi

Avinguda del Paral.lel

Ronda de Sant Pau

Gra Teat del Li

Fundació Joan Miró

Estadi Olímpic de Montjuïc

Avinguda de Miramar

Funicular

Carrer Nou de la Rambla

Carrer Nou de la Rambla

Avda. de les Drassanes

Telefèric

Reials Drassanes (Museu Marítim)

Plaça del Portal de la Pau

Montjuïc

Castell de Montjuïc

Carrer de Miramar

Moll Sant Bertran

Torre de Jaume

Moll de Barcelona

Worl Trade Cente

Ronda Litoral

BARCELONA

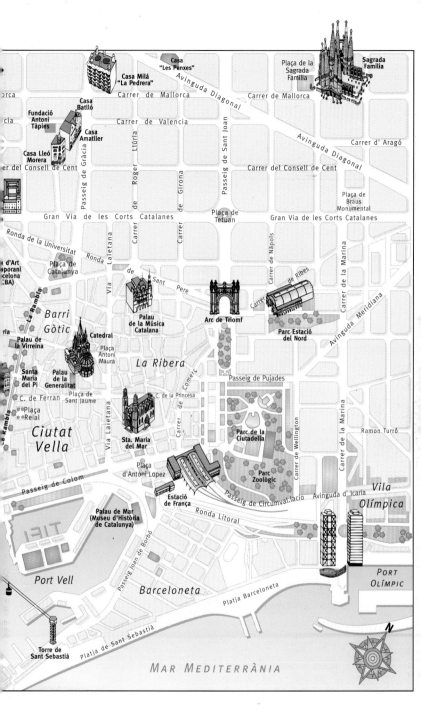

Sagrada Família

Plaça de la Sagrada Família

Casa "Les Punxes"

Casa Milà "La Pedrera"

Avinguda Diagonal

Carrer de Mallorca

Carrer de Mallorca

Fundació Antoni Tàpies

Casa Batlló

Carrer de Valencia

Casa Amatller

Carrer d' Aragó

Casa Lleó Morera

Avinguda Diagonal

er del Consell de Cent

Carrer del Consell de Cent

Passeig de Gràcia

Carrer de Roger de Llúria

Carrer de Girona

Passeig de Sant Joan

Plaça de Braus Monumental

Gran Via de les Corts Catalanes

Plaça de Tetuan

Gran Via de les Corts Catalanes

Carrer de Nàpols

Carrer de la Marina

Ronda de la Universitat

Via Laietana

Ronda de Sant Pere

d'Art poraní celona BA)

Plaça de Catalunya

Carrer de Ribes

Carrer de la Marina

Avinguda Meridiana

Barri Gòtic

Palau de la Música Catalana

Arc de Triomf

Parc Estació del Nord

Catedral

ria

Palau de la Virreina

Plaça Antoni Maura

La Ribera

Passeig de Pujades

Santa Maria del Pi

Palau de la Generalitat

Plaça de Sant Jaume

C. de la Princesa

Carrer de Comerç

Parc de la Ciutadella

Carrer de Wellington

Carrer de la Marina

C. de Ferran

Ciutat Vella

Plaça Reial

Via Laietana

Sta. Maria del Mar

Ramon Turró

a Rambla

Plaça d'Antoni Lopez

Parc Zoològic

Vila Olímpica

Passeig de Colom

Estació de França

Passeig de Circumval.lació

Avinguda d' Icaria

Palau de Mar (Museu d'Història de Catalunya)

Ronda Litoral

Port Vell

Passeig de Joan de Borbó

Barceloneta

Platja Barceloneta

PORT OLÍMPIC

Torre de Sant Sebastià

Platja de Sant Sebastià

MAR MEDITERRÀNIA

N

Barri Gòtic

While the *Barri Gòtic*, also known as "Barri de la Seu" (Cathedral quarter) or by the odd name of "rovell de l'ou" (egg yolk), may not be a district in the true sense of the word, it does enclose most of what remains of medieval Barcelona and includes some of the most interesting monuments in the city. Extending from the City Hall to the Cathedral and encircled by the bastions of the Roman walls, it is probably the most fascinating area of the city. The name of Gothic Quarter came into use in the early 20th century when it was realised that, although it is not the only Gothic area of the city, the complex of buildings remaining here is more harmonious and therefore deserving of greater attention as indeed has been the case with the extensive restoration work that has been carried out in the area.

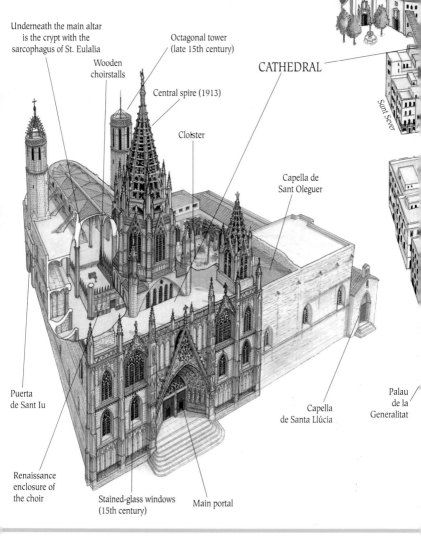

Underneath the main altar is the crypt with the sarcophagus of St. Eulalia

Wooden choirstalls

Octagonal tower (late 15th century)

CATHEDRAL

Central spire (1913)

Cloister

Capella de Sant Oleguer

Sant Sever

Puerta de Sant Iu

Capella de Santa Llúcia

Palau de la Generalitat

Renaissance enclosure of the choir

Stained-glass windows (15th century)

Main portal

Casa de l'Ardiaca

Museu
Frederic Marès

Palau
Reial Major

Roman
walls

Saló
del Tinell

Monument to Ramón
Berenguer on horseback

Carrer de la

Tapineria

Santa Llúcia

Carrer

Plaça de
Ramón
Berenguer III

dels Comtes

Plaça
del Rei

Carrer

de Barcelona

del Bisbe

Carrer de Jaume I

Carrer de la Ciutat

Museu
d'Història
de la Ciutat

Casa de la Ciutat
(Ajuntament)

Palau de
Lloctinent

13

THE "GOTHIC QUARTER" - The *Barri Gòtic* begins in the *Plaça Nova,* the oldest square of Barcelona where, in the 13th-century, one of the most flourishing markets in the city was held and slaves were once sold. Two Roman towers that formed part of the old city walls and constituted the city's only defense until the 13th century are still to be found here. The ***Palau Episcopal*** (Bishop's Palace) which rises to the right of the Roman towers also dates to the 13th century and creates an interesting contrast with the modern ***Collegio d'Arquitectes*** (College of Architects), decorated on the outside with a graffito frieze designed by Picasso. To the left of the Roman towers is another interesting building, the ***Casa de l'Ardiaca*** (at present seat of the historical Archives of the City and the Historical Institute of Barcelona), which takes its name from the fact that it was the residence of the archdeacon Lluís Desplá. The building, which probably dates from the 11th century, was restructured throughout the centuries and is a harmonious fusion of Gothic and renaissance styles. One of the three façades of the palace looks out on the ***Carrer del Bisbe Irurita*** (Bishop Street), the heart of the *Barri Gòtic,* which skirts the side of the Cathedral and ends in *Plaça de Sant-Jaume.* About halfway along, this lovely street is crossed by a charming suspended bridge connecting the *Palau de la Generalitat* to the second façade of the ***Casa dels Canonges*** (Canons' House). This recently-restored 14th century building faces onto the *Carrer Paradís.* Various medieval buildings here that are open to the public house the Centro Excursionista de Cataluña and the remains of a **Roman Temple** dedicated to Augustus dating from the 2nd century. The four imposing Corinthian columns are topped by an architrave and stand on a podium. The temple was built on the highest and most important point of the ancient *Barcino,* on the highest point of the *Mons Taber.* On the right of the *Carrer del Bisbe Irurita,* before reaching the bridge, is a narrow lane which leads to the most intimate, hidden little square in the city. *Plaça de Sant Felip Neri* is one of the most peaceful spots in the city with a simple fountain at the centre and dominated by the sober 18th-century **Church of Sant Felip Neri**. The building housing the *Museum of the History of Shoe-making* (*Museu del Calçat Antic y el Gremi de Calderers*) also faces onto the small square.

CATHEDRAL OF SAINT EULALIA

In the 4th century a small church already stood on the highest point of the old Roman colony, the small *Mons Taber*. And it must have been an important church if two centuries later, as the Cathedral of Barcelona, it was the setting for the Council of 559. These were times of violence and the church was destroyed by Almanzor in 985. Shortly after the year 1000, the Catalan Count Ramón Berenguer I rebuilt it in Romanesque style, but plans for the great church which today rises next to the *Avinguda de la Catedral,* in the heart of the *Barri Gòtic,* were only begun under

Cathedral façade with the main entrance.

James II, king of Aragon. Construction began in 1298 and continued until 1448 following the stylistic canons of Catalan Gothic. An inscription near the *Puerta de Sant Iu* in *Carrer dels Comtes* commemorates the date the work was begun. The Cathedral was dedicated to Saint Eulalia, a legendary young girl who was tortured and killed for her Christian faith in the 4th century. Over the years the building has undergone considerable modification. The main façade of the church dates to the end of the 19th century and was quite controversial. The architects, Mestres and Font, were supposed to have followed the original designs of 1408 by a French architect. The central spire of the cathedral was not built until 1913. The interior is grandiose and austere. The stained-glass windows date to the 15th century and illuminate the nave and two aisles which represent Catalan Gothic at its purest. The Cathedral is a real treasure trove: the 26 chapels, the sacristy, the crypt with the sarcophagus of the Saint, the lovely cloister – all should be attentively visited. On one side of the main entrance is the **Capella del Baptisteri,** with marble baptismal fonts, by Onofre Julia, dated 1443. On the other side is the large **Capella de Sant Oleguer** protected by a wrought iron railing dated 1405. Above Bishop Oleguer's altar is a 16th-century wooden *Crucifix* by Ça-Anglada, which Don Juan of Austria carried on the flagship of the Christian fleet in the battle of Lepanto. Beyond the *Capella de Sant Oleguer* is the **Capella de Sant Climent**, with the Gothic sepulchre of Doña Sança Ximenis de Cabrera and a 15th-century altarpiece. The presbytery, the **Capella Major** (Chancel) of the Cathedral, opens off the transept. In the other chapels opening off the central transept are numerous

An impressive view of the graceful Gothic vaults in the Cathedral. In the foreground is the renaissance enclosure of the Choir.

14th and 15th-century altarpieces, magnificent examples of Catalan art. The 15th-century altarpiece of the *Visitation* is in the **Capella de Sant Miquel,** and one of Bernat Martorell's masterpieces, the altarpiece of the *Transfiguration,* is in the **Capella del Patrocini,** while the 14th-century altarpiece of the *Archangel Gabriel* is in the apse, the **Capella del Santíssim Sacrament**. The sixth chapel contains the altarpiece of *Saints Martin and Ambrose* and the seventh, a mid-15th century altarpiece representing *Saint Claire and Saint Catherine.* The Gothic sepulchre of Bishop Ramón de Escales is to be found in the **Capella dels Sants I-nocents**. The two sepulchres of the founders of the Cathedral, Count Ramón Berenguer I and his wife Almodis, are to be seen to the right of the high altar. To the left of the transept, the **Puerta de Sant Iu,** the oldest part of the Cathedral which is still Romanesque in appearance, leads to the *Carrer dels Comtes.* Under the Capella Major, a short flight of stairs leads to the **Crypt** where the body of Saint Eulalia is preserved in an *alabaster sarcophagus* of 1327, the work of a pupil of the Italian sculptor Nicola Pisano. The German artist Müller painted the *Incoronation of Saint Eulalia* on the large keystone of the vault of the Crypt, which was designed by Jaime Fabré. The renaissance enclosure of the large **Choir** is at the centre of the nave. Work on the construction began in 1390 when Ramón de Escales was bishop of Barcelona, and his coat of arms (three ladders) is sculpted on the walls of the Choir. The entire enclosure is decorated with marble bas-reliefs which narrate the life of

SANT'EULALIA

Both Barcelona and Merida lay claim to Eulalia who was born around 290 A.D. At the time of the persecutions carried out by the emperor Diocletian, though just 14 years old, she did not hesitate to proclaim her devout belief in Christ in public. The young girl was therefore destined to be martyred and, after being put to torture with Saint Julia she was burnt at the stake in Merida. She is now celebrated on two different days: Saint Eulalia of Merida on 10 December and as Saint Eulalia of Barcelona on 12 February.
The identification of these two personages in the one saint is still controversial.

17

The magnificent choir stalls showing a detail of the wealth of elegant gilded and polychrome decoration.

Saint Eulalia, begun in 1517 by Bartolome Ordoñez. Inside are the famous wooden stalls, decorated with gilded polychrome coats of arms of the Knights of the Order of the Golden Fleece who were convoked in the Cathedral by Emperor Charles V and archduke Maximilian of Austria in 1519. The upper stalls and the bishop's throne are by Ça-Anglada, and the crowning canopy of the stalls was created by the German artist Lochner and completed at the end of the 15th century. In a corner, to the right of the Capella Major, is the **Sacristy** which houses the *Cathedral Treasury*. This valuable collection of liturgical objects and religious art includes a 15th-century reliquary decorated with the collar of the Order of the Golden Fleece which belonged to Charles V, the gilded chair of the Aragonese King Martin I and a gold and silver monstrance of 1390. Access to the **Cloister** is through the *Puerta de Sant Sever*, inside the church, from the Chapel of Saint Lucy, to the right of the main entrance to the cathedral; from the **Puerta de Santa Eulàlia**, (Gate of St. Eulalia), an attractive entrance in flamboyant Gothic style dating from the 15th century and incomplete, which opens onto the *Carrer del Bisbe Irurita*; and through the **Puerta de la Pietat** in the *carrer* of the same name, decorated in the lunette above the portal with a wooden carved *Pietà* in northern European style (16th century). The cloister, which is without doubt one of the loveliest Gothic cloisters in existence, is unique due to the diversity of its components. The old chapels of the religious congregations, separated from the cloister portico by austere wrought iron railings, open off three of its four sides. The wing set against the side of the Cathedral is the oldest and dates to the 14th century, while the others are mid-15th century. Where the oldest wing and the wing perpendicular to the side of the church meet is the Romanesque **Puerta de Sant Sever**, in front of which is a charming old convent lavabo set at the centre of a sort of small temple, the **Pabelló de Sant Jordi**, with the vault decorated with sculpture representing *St. George* at the centre and the *Fathers of the Church* on the ribs. Every year for the feast day of Corpus Christi, the traditional *ou com balla* (dancing egg) is held: an eggshell which "dances" suspended above the basin of the washstand on its spout of water. Near the temple is a small pond and a flock of geese, which some say are symbols of Saint Eulalia's purity. In the corner diagonally opposite the *Puerta de Sant Sever* are the remains of the 15th century Romanesque **Capella de Santa Llúcia**. Consecrated to the Madonna in 1268, the façade boasts a fine Romanesque portal. Inside is the tomb of the bishop Arnau de Gurb, founder of the chapel, and that of the parish priest of Santa Coloma. A picture of the saint is on the high altar. The **Chapter Hall**, adjoining the chapel, dates to the first half of the 15th century and houses the *Cathedral Museum*, with a collection that includes the famous *Pietà* by Bartolomé Bermejo (15th-century), the illuminated missal of Saint Eulalia (by Rafael Destorrents), the *altarpiece of St Bernardine* (15th-century) by Jaume Huguet the *Madonna and Child* (15th-century) by Sano di Pietro and *St Honoratius* (14th-century) by Jaime Serra.

The refined Gothic portico around the Cloister. Right: the ancient lavabo protected by Pabelló de Sant Jordi.

PALAU DE LA GENERALITAT

Plaça de Sant-Jaume is a sort of continuation of what was once the forum of the Roman city. Even today, following this tradition, the most important government buildings of Barcelona are found here: the *Palau de la Generalitat*, built in various phases, beginning in the 15th century, to house the *Diputación de Catalunya* (or Parliament) and the *Casa de la Ciutat* or *Ajuntament* (the City Hall). The main façade of the *Palau de la Generalitat*, a building in renaissance style by Pere Blai, dates to the late 16th century. The elegant secondary façade of 1416 is in Gothic style. It faces onto the lovely *Carrer del Bisbe Irurita* and is the work of the architect Marc Safont. But the finest part of the building is the ancient internal *courtyard*, access to which is through a wide depressed arch. It too is built in the Catalan Gothic style by Safont (1425) and is a perfect example of the aristocratic patio of the period. A staircase, supported by a single arch and with a finely decorated balustrade, leads to the main floor of the building where a loggia of ogival arches on slender columns looks out on the courtyard. A bold architectural solution has been found for the corner at the top of the staircase: two rounded arches (instead of pointed arches) are set side by side, separated only by a capital without a column which, like a stalactite, is suspended in the void. Once past this fascinating entrance we come face to face with the admirable **Capella de Sant Jordi** (Chapel of St. George), also by Safont (1432). The loggia of the main floor leads to the **Saló de Sant Jordi**, realized at the end

Above: the sombre main façade of the Palau de la Generalitat; below, the 19th century neoclassic façade of the Ajuntament.

of the 16th century by Pere Blai, which occupies the central part of the palace. It is a vast room with three aisles and vaults, supported by square pilasters, and with a dome at the centre decorated with frescoes of historical subjects executed in the 1920s by Josep Mongrell. The courtyard loggia also leads to the famous **Pati dels Tarongers** (Orange Tree Courtyard) executed between 1526 and 1600 and a good example of the transition from Gothic to renaissance architecture. It in turn leads to the *Saló del Consistori Major* or *Saló Daurat* (Gilded Hall), so-called because of the gilded ceiling. The wooden coffers of the ceiling also contain the carved and painted portraits of the Catalan kings.

AJUNTAMENT

The neoclassic façade of the palace is the result of 19th-century renovation of the original Gothic building. On one side, in the *Carrer de la Ciutat,* the old Gothic façade realized at the end of the 14th century by Arnau Barguès, can still be seen. The entrance portal is marked by a fine arch in relief which, on the right "trespasses" into a wing of the palace that is at right angles to the façade, creating an original aesthetic solution. Above the arch are the coats of arms of Barcelona and Catalonia and a statue of the *archangel Raphael*. The **Saló de Cent** is on the main floor of the building. It was created by Pere Llobet for the City Council of the Hundred in the 14th century and was inaugurated during the session of August 17, 1373 and enlarged in the mid-19th century. Access to the 19th-century *Saló de Sessions* where the City Council normally meets is from here. The chamber is also known as the *Saló de la Reina Regent,* the Hall of the Queen Regent, after the portrait of *Queen Maria Cristina with her son,* the young Alfonso XIII, located there. The main floor also contains the evocative *Saló de les Cròniques* of the first half of the century, almost completely frescoed by Josep Sert with historical scenes.

Above, a detail of the old Gothic façade of the Ajuntament with an elegant doorway, and right, a view of the Saló de Cent.

21

PLAÇA DE RAMÓN BERENGUER EL GRAN - *Plaça de Ramón Berenguer el Gran,* at the eastern edge of the city walls that are incorporated into the royal palace, creates a sort of narrow garden at the foot of the walls. Here, in *Via Laietana,* stands the *Equestrian Monument to Count-King Ramón Berenguer III* (1097-1131), a member of the same family that reconstructed the city's Cathedral in 1058. The monument is set against the backdrop of the Roman walls and the side of the **Capella de Santa Agata**. This palatine chapel of the Palau Reial Major stands on the site of an old oratory of Santa Maria and was built on the old Roman walls. The single high nave, with a series of ogival arches, has a fine polychrome wooden coffered ceiling.
The coats of arms of James II and his wife Blanche of Anjou can still be seen in the apse and one of the masterpieces of Catalan painting is set above the high altar, the altarpiece representing the *Adoration of the Magi* (at centre, below) and the *Crucifixion* (at centre, above), surrounded by six stories. The altarpiece was painted by Jaume Huguet in 1464 and is known as *"Retablo del Condestable"* because it was commissioned by the Constable Don Pedro of Portugal, one of the pretenders to the crown of Catalonia-Aragon. *Via Laietana* is one of the most important urban arteries of the city; crossing the oldest quarter of Barcelona it joins the "old town" to the harbour.
In the evening the panorama from here is spectacular: the majestic complex of the walls and of the Chapel of Saint Agatha, with the Mirador and the bell tower of the Cathedral rising up over them, are brightly illuminated and form a fantastic backdrop.

The Plaça de Ramón Berenguer el Gran with, in the foreground, an Equestrian Monument to the Count.

MUSEU D'HISTÒRIA DE LA CIUTAT

Opened in 1973, the museum is housed in the *Casa Clariana-Padellàs*, a 15th-century Gothic palace, which was transported stone by stone to its present site when *Via Laietana* was opened. In 1931 when excavations were made for new foundations, important remains of the old Roman city came to light. The discovery furnished the pretext for using the building as the Historical Museum of the City. In the vaults, which extend as far as the *Plaça de l'Angel*, the remains of the ancient Roman colony can be seen, with the old Roman forum (2nd century), a bathing establishment, a reproduction of the Visigothic necropolis, drainage canals. The remains of a 4th-century Christian basilica are also to be found in the vaults of *Carrer dels Comtes*.

Since 1999 this museum has been part of the City of Barcelona's ambitious project to reorganise its historical collections in order to improve access to the historical and artistic inhertiance while also preserving the artefacts and buildings that are evidence of its past. Thus, as well as housing

plans and panoramas of the city today, archaeological remains, photographs of the Gothic district, various paintings and prints, portraits, antique books and sarcophagi, this central museum is also linked to other important collections such as the *Museu Monestir de Pedralbes*, the *Casa-Museu Verdaguer* and the *Centre d'Intrepretació i Acollida del Parc Güell*.

The Museu d'Historia de la Cuidad has interesting artefacts (statues, bas-reliefs, fragments of buildings, etc.) of the old Roman city.

PALAU DEL LLOCTINENT - The majestic *Plaça del Rei* once the central part of the *Palau Reial Major,* residence first of the counts of Barcelona and then of the kings of Aragon, is at the very centre of the city's Gothic district. Facing onto the square are the *Palau del Lloctinent,* the tower known as **Mirador del Rei Martí** (a fascinating building dating from the middle of the 16th century with five superimposed galleries), the **Saló del Tinell** (the great hall of the palace of the counts, 14th-century), the **Capella de Santa Agata** (the 14th-century Palatine chapel) and the 16th-century **Casa Clariana-Padellàs** in which the *Historical Museum of the City* is located. The Palace of the Lieutenant or Viceroy, the secondary façade of which overlooks the square, is a sober building erected by Antoni Carbonell in 1549. It contains the *Archives of the Crown of Aragon,* over 4 million documents, dating back as far as the 9th century. Worthy of note is the characteristic patio with several orders of loggias and the airy main staircase, with its splendid coffered ceiling.

THE ROMAN WALLS - The *Barri Gòtic,* contrary to expectations, does not consist only of buildings that date to the 13th and 14th centuries, for considerable Roman remains dating back to the 4th century A.D. are to be found in their midst. The remains in question are what is left of the city walls built by the Romans after having reconquered the old "Barcino" which had been occupied and destroyed by the Barbarians in the second half of the 3rd century A.D. These walls, which were 1,270 metres long, were about 9 metres high, 3.50 meters thick and had sturdy polygonal towers and entrance gates set at intervals. The remains of a basilical building of the same period as the walls have been brought to light under the Cathedral and part of the initial structure of a Roman acqueduct, as well as a section of walls are visible in the Cathedral square. Remains of the ancient city walls can still be seen in *Carrer Correu Vell, Baixada Caçador Carrer Sostinent Navarro, Plaça de l'Angel, Baixada Llibreteria, Carrer Tapineria, Plaça de Ramón Berenguer el Gran,* and *Carrer dels Comtes,* which skirts the side of the Cathedral.

Above, the sombre façade of Palau Lloctinent. Right, a section of the imposing Roman walls.

MUSEU FREDERIC MARÈS

This museum is in an annex of the *Palau Reial Major* which consists of various buildings completed in different periods. Formerly the residence of the counts of Barcelona, it became the seat of the Holy Office in the second half of the 15th century. Subsequently it became the residence of the kings of Aragon and Castille, and Christopher Columbus was received there upon his return from the New World. During the 17th century the older wing was turned into a convent, today housing the *Museu Marès*.

The initial core of the collections belonged to the sculptor Frederic Marès i Deulovol, who donated it to the city of Barcelona in 1940. The exhibitions deal particularly with medieval sculpture, not only Catalan, but also from other regions of Spain. The collections on the ground floor of the museum provide a panorama from ancient Iberian, Greek and Punic works to 15th-century Castilian statuary and Aragonese sculpture. Of particular interest is a rich collection of *Crucifixes* of the 14th-15th centuries and one of enamelled or painted *Crosses* in wood or metal from the Gothic period to the 17th century. The sculpture and painting exhibited on the first floor range from the early Middle Ages to the 19th century. The *Madonna and Child* was a common theme in 15th-century sculpture while the *Holy Family* appears often in 13th to 16th-century works. The examples of Spanish renaissance sculpture clearly reveal Italian and Flemish influences. Particularly interesting from this point of view is a group of sculptures in alabaster (reliefs representing the *Annunciation,* the *Visitation,* the *Adoration of the Shepherds* and the *Presentation in the Temple,* by Francisco Giralte) and a *Virgin and Child* attributed to Alonso Berruguete.

FREDERIC MARÉS I DEULOVOL

Barcelona today owes much to this engaging character, who was born in 1893 and died almost a century later in 1991. A good sculptor he devoted much of his time to collecting rare examples of Spanish sculpture from the medieval period right up to the beginning of the 20th century. He thus succeeded in creating a magnificent collection that is unequalled in Spain but also helped to place schools, artists and masterpieces in a wider and more complete historic and artistic perspective.

Two suberb wooden sculptures of religious subjects, preserved in the Museu Marès.

SANTA MARÍA DEL PI - Also known as *Nuestra Señora de los Reyes* and rising on the site of a religious building of the 10th century, construction of the church began in 1322 and it was consecrated in 1453, although the crypt is 16th-century. A large rose window composed of fine modern polychrome stained glass stands out against the simple Gothic façade. **Inside,** a single wide nave flanked by chapels preserves a tomb dated 1394. The church stands on one side of the square where occasionally an attractive little market is held. The entire area around the church – the well-known 'Pino' quarter – is full of cafés, bars and pastry shops, often housed in quaint old buildings, antique shops or boutiques which deal in specialized products such as masks, maps, etc. A walk along *Carrer Petritxol* offers you the chance of savouring some of the city's most delicious specialities.

SANTS JUST I PASTOR - This ancient church, mentioned in sources as early as 801, is situated on *Plaça Sant Just* together with several other Gothic buildings. The church as it is now

---

PALAU REQUESENS

Not far from the church of Sants Just i Pastor is one of the most important aristo-cratic residences of Bar-celona, *Palau Requesens*, built in the 16th century for Lluís de Requesens, a close and faithful friend of Philip II. Restored in 1970, the palace now houses the *Reial Acadèmia de les Bones Lletres* (promoting an awareness of Catalan history and literature since 1790) and the *Galeria de Catalanes Ilustres*, a collection of images of famous Catalonians since the 10th century.

Above, Santa María del Pi, showing the austere and elegant Gothic façade. Left, the ancient church of Sants Just i Pastor.

dates back to the 14th-15th century. The simple façade is flanked by only one of the two bell towers originally planned. **Inside**, a single nave has side chapels decorated with reliefs. In the Chapel of St Felix is an altarpiece representing the saint. An estimable work by the Portuguese Pedro Núñez it dates to the first half of the 16th century. According to the city statutes of 1282, the Church of Sants Just i Pastor has the power to concede the privilege "de los Testamentos Sacramentales" (The Right of Sacramental Wills), which is still valid and according to which the last will of a dying person, verbally pronounced, becomes legally valid, even in the absence of written documents, if it is repeated, under oath and within six months, before the altar in the chapel of San Felix, by the witnesses present when it was formulated.

CARRER DE MONTCADA - *Carrer Princesa,* a street off *Via Laietana,* leads to *Carrer de Montcada,* originally little more than a path along the banks of a brook, but honoured with the name of "Calle Nueva" when the first buildings began to rise just outside the old city walls. The present name derives from Guillem Ramon de Montcada who built his palace there in 1153. From the 13th until the 18th century this street was one of the most aristocratic in the city, with rich mansions built along either side. Its splendour came to an end in the 19th-century when the high society of the time preferred other areas of Barcelona.

PALAU DEL MARQUES DE LLIÓ

One of the old houses that still stands in this street at no. 12, is the majestic Palau del Marques de Llió, a fine 14th century building, now owned by the city and housing the *Museu Tèxtil i de la Indumentaria* (Costume Museum), a generous bequest of Manuel Rocamora. The three floors of this elegant palace contain exhibitions of liturgical vestment, dolls, shoes, costume accessories (fans and purses), matador costumes, tapestries, uniforms, examples of fine embroidery. The oldest objects date to the 16th century, and the most recent are 20th-century.

The severe yet majestic 14th century courtyard of Palau del Marques de Llió, now a large and interesting Costume Museum.

MUSEU BARBIER-MUELLER D'ART PRECOLOMBI

Opened in 1997 by Queen Sofia in a building of medieval origin, *Palau Nadal* at no. 14 *Carrer de Montcada*, this interesting museum has one of the largest and most important collections of Pre-Colombian art in the world. The 6,000 items of immense value, presented to the city of Barcelona by the Barbier-Mueller Museum in Geneva, represent the incomparable result of the genuine passion of Josef Mueller (1887-1977) who began a small but important

Arts of the Americas, Mexico, Chupicuaro, Female Figure, painted ceramic, 500-100 B.C., Museu Barbier-Mueller, Pierre-Alain Ferrazzini Collection.

Arts of the Americas, Central Region, Maya, Funerary Mask in fuchsine, c. 400 A.D., Museu Barbier-Mueller, Pierre-Alain Ferrazzini Collection.

Arts of the Americas, Brazil, Island of Marajo,
Large Ceramic Funerary Urn, c. 1000 A.D., Museu
Barbier-Mueller, Pierre-Alain Ferrazzini Collection.

collection of ancient tribal artefacts in 1908. Exhibited are ceramic items, stone sculptures, jade figurines and funerary artefacts both religious or more simply decorative. In this splendid and eclectic variety of styles, materials and colours all the main pre-colombian cultures of Mesoamerica, Andean America and Amazzonia are represented, ranging from the Mayans to the Olmecs of the Gulf of Mexico, whose majestic and spectacular creations date from the first millenium B.C.

29

MUSEU PICASSO

The **Palau Berenguer d'Aguilar,** a 14th-century building with a fine Gothic patio, is at no. 15 *Carrer de Montcada.* The

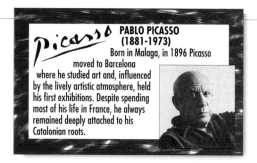

PABLO PICASSO
(1881-1973)
Born in Malaga, in 1896 Picasso moved to Barcelona where he studied art and, influenced by the lively artistic atmosphere, held his first exhibitions. Despite spending most of his life in France, he always remained deeply attached to his Catalonian roots.

palace was the residence of the Llinás family and then of the counts of Santa Coloma who modified the original Gothic structure of the building in renaissance and Baroque style. It is now the home of the *Museu Picasso,* and the three floors are given over to the donation of Jaume Sabartés, a friend of the painter, and the donation Picasso himself made, consisting of several hundred oil paintings, sketches, drawings and etchings. The space was insufficient for all these works and the collection overflowed into the *Palau Baró de Castellet,* a 17th-century building, as well as the *Palau Meca* at no. 19. In 1999 a further development linked the museum to the 18th century *Casa Mauri* and *Palau Finestres* which house temporary exhibitions. The quantity and variety of the material exhibited (arranged chronologically) make this museum a unique and indispensable instrument to understand the work of the great artist – from one of his first attempts (a drawing done when he was nine years old) to the works painted towards the end of the century, in La Coruña, the production from his two sojourns in Barcelona (from 1895 to 1897 and from 1901 to 1904), the famous "blue period" (after his stay in Paris), his cubist experiments,

up to the paintings done in Cannes in 1957. To mention only a few of the masterpieces here, there is the large oil painting, *Science and Charity,* done by the master when he was barely fifteen, *El Paseo Colón* and *Barcelona* (dedicated to the city he loved so much), *El Niño Enfermo* (blue period) and *Harlequin* (1917, cubist period). A whole section of the museum is dedicated to the 58 paintings which Picasso donated to the museum in 1968, 44 of which are variations on the theme of *Las Meninas,* the famous painting by Velázquez in the Prado.

Pablo Ruiz Picasso,
Harlequin of Barcelona,
oil on canvas, cm. 116X90,
1917.

Above, Pablo Ruiz Picasso, Mother and Child, *pastel and charcoal on paper, cm. 46X40, 1903.*

Below, one of the 44 varations on the theme of Las Meninas *by Velázquez which Picasso donated to the museum in 1968.*

31

The typically baroque courtyard of Palau Dalmasas. Below, Santa María del Mar: an evocative nocturnal view of the upper part of the façade, with the rose window and the slender octagonal towers.

PALAU DALMASES - Continuing along *Carrer de Montcada,* the *Palau Dalmases* at no. 20 is one of those aristocratic residences which help to make this street so charming. Even if it is not perfectly preserved, the 17th-century palace with its fine Baroque patio and family chapel with relief decoration in the vault, is still quite splendid. Built as the residence of Pau Ignasi de Dalmases, it was later also the seat of the "Academia dels Desconfiats" (Academy of the Diffident).

SANTA MARÍA DEL MAR - The apse of the church of *Santa María del Mar* lies at the end of *Carrer de Montcada*. The church is one of the most important examples of medieval Catalan architec-

A view of the interior of Santa María del Mar showing its austere simplicity.

ture and both it and the *carrer* have been declared national monuments. In the first half of the 14th century, after having occupied Sardinia, Alfonso IV initiated the building of the church to absolve a vow previously made by James I. The architect Berenguer de Montagut built it on the site of an earlier parish church of the 10th century, and work was completed under Peter IV, in 1383. The exterior of the church is majestic with its wide plain surfaces, a fine splayed portal, harmonious tall ogival windows and two slender octagonal bell towers crowned by three orders of windows. The lovely flamboyant Gothic rose window which decorates the upper part of the façade is the result of a revision carried out in the second half of the 15th century after the original window had been destroyed by the dreadful earthquake of 1428. Stylistically the nave and two narrow aisles of the **interior** are unusually unified and are supported by octagonal piers. These are so few that they are 13 metres apart, a surprisingly large interval for Gothic cathedrals, constituting one of the most particular features of the building. Some of the elegant 15th-century stained-glass windows are also noteworthy (the *Last Judgement* in the left aisle, the *Assumption of the Virgin* in one of the side chapels and, above all, the *Coronation of the Virgin* at the centre of the rose window on the façade).

Unfortunately the fire of 1936 almost completely destroyed the decoration of the interior and the high altar, a fine Baroque work of the second half of the 18th century.

LAS RAMBLAS

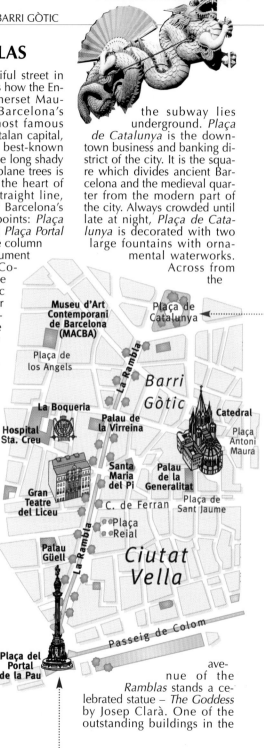

"The most beautiful street in the world". This is how the English writer Somerset Maugham defined Barcelona's *Ramblas*, the most famous avenue in the Catalan capital, and perhaps the best-known in all of Spain. The long shady street lined with plane trees is a promenade in the heart of the old city, a straight line, that joins two of Barcelona's most important points: *Plaça de Catalunya* and *Plaça Portal de la Pau* with the column bearing the monument to Christopher Columbus. In the *Ramblas* traffic runs along either side of a wide pavement where one can freely walk, rest, play, talk. *Plaça de Catalunya* is the most famous and best loved square in the city, the strategic nerve centre of Barcelona. Nine of the city's principal streets meet here while the subway lies underground. *Plaça de Catalunya* is the downtown business and banking district of the city. It is the square which divides ancient Barcelona and the medieval quarter from the modern part of the city. Always crowded until late at night, *Plaça de Catalunya* is decorated with two large fountains with ornamental waterworks. Across from the avenue of the *Ramblas* stands a celebrated statue – *The Goddess* by Josep Clarà. One of the outstanding buildings in the

Museu d'Art Contemporani de Barcelona (MACBA)

Plaça de Catalunya

Plaça de los Angels

La Rambla

Barri Gòtic

La Boqueria

Palau de la Virreina

Catedral

Hospital Sta. Creu

Plaça Antoni Maura

Santa Maria del Pi

Palau de la Generalitat

Gran Teatre del Liceu

C. de Ferran

Plaça de Sant Jaume

Plaça Reial

Palau Güell

La Rambla

Ciutat Vella

Passeig de Colom

Plaça del Portal de la Pau

Two views of the beautiful and elegant Plaça de Catalunya, with one of the two large fountains. Below, colour, flowers, creativity and streets that are always busy – this is the usual image of the Ramblas.

vicinity of the avenue of the *Ramblas* is the Romanesque-Gothic church of **Santa Ana**, built in 1146 and restored after it was destroyed by fire in 1936. Inside is an elegant galleried *cloister* dating to the 14th-15th century. The avenues of the *Ramblas* are over a kilometer long (1,180 metres). The trees were planted during the Napoleonic occupation by General Duchesne who had them brought from Gerona. The *Ramblas* lie on the bed of a river which the Arabs named "Ram-la" and which marked the boundary of the medieval stronghold. A second circle of walls was built around old Barcelona along the course of the stream. In the course of time, mainly religious buildings were erected along the banks of the "Ram-la" and what was later to become the *Ramblas* was at the time known as the *Calle de los Conventos*. It was not until 1704 that what was left of the stream began to be covered up and urbanized and that the *Ramblas* began to take on their present aspect.

Ramblear – a neologism which means "to stroll along the Ramblas" - is one of the favorite pastimes of the Barcelonians. To walk slowly up and down this long boulevard, back and forth between *Plaça de Catalunya* and the port, stopping to discuss football (around the *Font de Canaletes*) or corrida (at the *Arco del Teatro*) is how the inhabitants of Barcelona love best to pass the time of day. The *Ramblas* are the heart and also the market of the city: newstands that look more like bookshops, cafés, vendors of flowers and birds, mime and street performers, sailors off duty populate this part of Barcelona at all hours of the day and night.

The *Ramblas* is actually a succession of avenues, five different streets with different names and each with distinct characters. The *Rambla de Canaletes* is the first part, right off *Plaça de Catalunya*. The lovely fountain almost at its beginning is magical. Legend says that whoever drinks its waters will never again leave Barcelona. The name of the old university which Philip V transferred to Cervera still exists in the second part of the *Ramblas*, the *Rambla dels Estudis*, now occupied by the cages of the bird vendors. The Baroque church of **Mare de Dèu de Betlem** (Church of Bethlehem,

18th-century) and the **Palau Moya** (late 18th-century) close the *Rambla dels Estudis*. The liveliest and loveliest part of the Ramblas begins here: the *Rambla de Sant Josep* now also baptized *Rambla de les Flors* because of the dozens of flower vendors to be found there. On either side is the popular **Mercat de la Boquería** (a colonnaded market with an iron roof) and the **Palau de la Virreina** which houses the *Museu–Gabinet Postal* and hosts temporary exhibitions. The *Pla de la Boquería*, a confusing and noisy intersection of the *Ramblas*, interrupts the *Rambla de les Flors* and is followed by the *Rambla dels Caputxins* where Barcelona's most important theatre stands – the **Gran Teatre del Liceu** next to the church of *San Pau del Camp*. *Calle Conde del Asalto*, to the right of the *Ramblas*, leads to **Palau Güell,** by Antoni Gaudí, which now houses the *Museu de les Arts de l'Espectacle* (Theatre Arts). This little street is one of those bordering the *Barri Xino* (the Chinese quarter).

The *Rambla de Santa Mónica* is the last part of the avenue and leads directly to the monumental column to Columbus, a few steps from the entrance to the port of Barcelona.

PALAU DE LA VIRREINA - Facing the *Rambla de les Flors*, the palace was commissioned in 1772 from the architect Carles Grau by the Viceroy of Peru, who died before it was completed in 1778. His wife, María Francisca de Fivaller, went to live there and the palace took its name from her, as vice-queen (*virreina*) of Peru. Today the palace is an exhibition centre and houses the *Gabinet Postal* and the *Gabinet Numismàtic* (collections of stamps and ancient and modern coins).

Above, the façade of Palau de la Virreina.
Centre, the emblem of the Boquería Market.
Below, the Gran Teatre del Liceu.

MERCAT DE LA BOQUERÍA - The *Boqueria* Market is without doubt one of the most famous and characteristic of Barcelona. Everything can be found here, from vegetables to fish, from fruit to the most unusual foods – and all as fresh as possible. Not to be missed are the vendors who are renowned for their chaotic and rowdy shouting, discussing their products with the customers and providing a amusing performance.

GRAN TEATRE DEL LICEU - One of the most famous theatres in the world, this is also one of the best in Europe as far as acoustics is concerned and second only to La Scala of Milan in its seating capacity. Originally begun in 1844 on the *Rambla dels Caputxins* on the site of the Monastery of *La Bona Nova* which was initially built in 1638, it was based on the plans of the architect Garriga i Roca. After a fire in 1861, the *Teatre del Liceu* was fully restored to its former splendour. In January 1994 it was once more entirely destroyed by fire but again with the determination and support of the authorities it has been laboriously and gloriously resurrected.

The Three Graces *decorate this fine fountain in the centre of elegant Plaça Reial.*

PLAÇA REIAL

In the heart of Barcelona's old city, surrounded by a series of classical arches, a row of austere palaces reflecting the influence of French Napoleonic architecture, palm trees in the paved squares, a fountain flanked by the *Three Graces, Plaça Reial* is the place to seek refuge from the rush and hubbub of the *Ramblas. Plaça Reial* was planned and built by Daniel Molina who also designed the houses with fine porticoes which surround the *Mercat de la Boquería,* on the other side of the *Ramblas.* The curious streetlamps are one of the early works of the great Antoni Gaudí. *Plaça Reial* is a particularly lively spot on Sundays when a philatelic and numismatic market attracts collectors, dealers and passers-by alike.

PALAU GÜELL - Palau Güell was designed and built by Antoni Gaudí between 1885 and 1890 for the Catalan industrialist Eusebi Güell and is today one of the buildings protected by UNESCO as a World Heritage Site. Its most original structure, the mosaics and chimneys make it an authentic symbol of Barcelona.

MUSEU DE CERA

In the immediate vicinity of the Portal de la Pau there is an interesting Wax Museum. This unusual, but famous collection exhibits a curious selection of personages all distinctly characteristic whether famous or less so, reproduced in wax. More than 300 figures can be admired in an attractive and suitably adapted setting.

PORTAL DE LA PAU

The Gateway of Peace (*Portal de la Pau*) is the natural outlet for the long avenues of the *Ramblas*, a large square which is one of the nerve centres of Barcelona. This square marks the boundary between the medieval city and the port and is at the crossing between *Passeig de Colom* and the *Avinguda del Paral·lel* on the street that rises to the castle of Montjuïc. The famous **Monument to Christopher Columbus**, one of the best-known symbols of the Catalan capital, rises at the centre of *Portal de la Pau*. The monument commemorates the return of the Italian navigator from the shores of the New World and his meeting, after his trip, with the Spanish sovereigns in Tinell Hall in the Royal Palace of Barcelona. But fate can be ironic – the discovery of America, favoured by a Catalan king, marked the beginning of the decline of the port of Barcelona. The monument was built at the end of the 19th century after designs by Gaieta Buigas. It was inaugurated late in the spring of 1888 and consists of an iron column about 51 metres high.

CHRISTOPHER COLOMBUS (1451-1506)

A navigator from Genoa who landed in the Bahamas in 1492 while serving the King of Spain. He died without knowing, however, that he had discovered a new continent.

Portrait of Christopher Colombus.

The statue of Columbus is in bronze and about 8 metres high. An elevator rises to the top of the column and permits a fine panorama of the port of Barcelona. Some of the most important buildings in the city are situated around

Plaça Portal de la Pau, showing the Monument to Christopher Columbus.

This was the period in which Barcelona dominated the Mediterranean, the golden age of Catalonia as a sea power. The royal shipyards worked full time for centuries: they were capable of building 30 sailing ships at a time. But with the discovery of America, the Catalan capi-

THE ROYAL ARSENAL

The *Drassanes*, the huge Royal Shipyards of the great medieval Catalan navy, are beside the *Portal de la Pau*. The original core of the building was constructed at the order of James I on the occasion of the war against the Saracens for the control of the Balearic Islands. The original building was enlarged by Peter III.

tal was excluded from the route to the New World and relegated to a secondary role. As time went by, the naval shipyards changed owner and function until 1941 when the city decided to create the *Maritime Museum* there. The immense rooms have permitted the reconstruction and exhibition of the flagship of the Christian fleet in the battle of Lepanto

(1571) against the Turks. The royal galley of Admiral Don Juan of Austria was built here in the shipyards of the Catalan capital. The replica was built in 1971, the year in which Barcelona celebrated the fourth centenary of its victory. The Maritime Museum collections also include archaeological finds, navigation charts, models of fishing boats and merchant ships, ceramics, original figureheads, and among its wealth of holdings, an atlas of 1493 which belonged to Amerigo Vespucci. Barceloneta, a seaside district that developed in the 18th century, forms the background to the port.

Maritime Museum: the reconstruction of the galley of Don Juan of Austria and a detail of the richly decorated sides.

the *Portal de la Pau*: behind the monument to Columbus is the *Royal Arsenal,* in which the **Maritime Museum** is housed, while the *Customs* offices are located on the opposite side of the square in a palace designed by the architect Enric Sagnier at the end of the 20th century. The *Palace of the Military Governor* and the port offices are also at the *Portal de la Pau*. At the entrance to the Paral-lel, which joins *Portal de la Pau* to *Plaça de Espanya,* is a section of the 15th-century walls, with the only extant gate of that part of the city walls: the *Porta de Santa Madrona.*

The impressive Customs' Buildings, dating from the end of the 19th century.

Hospital de la Santa
Creu i de Sant Pau: one
of the modern parts, and
the reading room of the
Biblioteca de Catalunya.

HOSPITAL DE LA SANTA CREU - The Hospital of the Holy Cross is an extraordinary ensemble of buildings in the heart of the old hospital district, not far from the *Ramblas* and now known as the *Hospital de la Santa Creu i de Sant Pau*. The first stone was laid in 1401 on a site where four hospitals, two civil and two religious, already stood. The complex was finished in 1415, enlarged in 1509 and rebuilt in 1638. At the end of the 15th century, with the new and demanding requirements of the city, more suitable quarters for the hospital were created (elegantly designed by L. Domènech i Montaner and financed by a bequest of the banker Pau Gil) and the original *Hospital de la Santa Creu* was used for the splendid *Biblioteca de Catalunya*.

SANT PAU DEL CAMP - According to some sources, a community of Benedictine monks lived in the fields which divided the heart of the old city from the hill of Montjuïc. Their monastery was probably destroyed during the years of Arab domination. The Romanesque church of *Sant Pau del Camp* was built on those ruins – one of the loveliest churches in Barcelona. While the main building dates back to 1117, the chapter hall and the abbot's house were built a century late, and the bell tower dates to the

Sant Pau del
Camp: the exterior
and a view of the
simple and
delightful
Romanesque
cloister.

La Llotja; the Gothic Transactions Hall with the magnificent coffered ceiling.

18th century. But the gem of the church is its delightful *cloister,* the loggia and garden of which are a peaceful refuge well-known to the Barcelonians.

LA LLOTJA - At the end of the *Passeig de Colom,* is the *Casa della Llotja,* once the home of the Stock Exchange and Academy of Fines Arts (attended by both Picasso and Miró) and now the Chamber of Commerce. The façade of the Llotja is by the architect J. Soler i Faneca, who redesigned the palace in neoclassic style in the second half of the 18th century. But the real history of the building begins in the 14th century with the original core, built between 1380 and 1390 as a covered market, the first building of its kind in all of Spain. In the 15th century it became the headquarters for the customs offices and the naval consulate. The large *Transactions Hall* is all that is left of the original structure. It is a fine example of the Gothic style, with three aisles and six arches which support the polychrome coffered wooden ceiling.

BASÍLICA DE LA MERCÈ - Close to the *Passeig de Colom* is a small church in Baroque style, built between 1765 and 1775 - the *Basílica de la Mercè.* Josep Mas, who designed it, utilized the old Gothic remains of the Church of San Miguel and preserved a renaissance side doorway dating to 1516. The basilica was actually the sanctuary of the Convent of the Brothers of Mercy and is now occupied by the *Capitanía General.* The *Basílica de la Mercè* is important for Barcelona because it preserves the sacred venerated image of the *Virgin of Mercy,* a small but elegant wooden statue, richly dressed in gold raiments, made in the 14th century by the wood sculptor Pere Moragues. The Virgin of Mercy, together with the "Moreneta" of Montserrat, is a protectress of Barcelona. At the end of September, with the arrival of autumn, the entire city celebrates its protectress in grandiose style. It is the finest holiday of the year, a joyous rite that is both secular and religious, extending well beyond the limits of the church and exploding into the streets and squares.

Basílica de la Mercè: the baroque façade and the much venerated wooden statue of the Virgin of Mercy, protectress of the city.

Don Quixote and Sancho Panza in the scene in Plaza de España, in Seville, painted on tiles.

MIGUEL DE CERVANTES SAAVEDRA (1547-1616)

A Spanish poet and writer, he was the author of the first modern novel *Don Quixote della Mancia* (1605-1615). The novel captures the atmosphere of an era, the Baroque period, when all the grand ideals of an age began to weaken and fade. His hero who continues to passionately defend his own principles, completely – and comically – looses contact with reality and humanity.

PASSEIG DE COLOM - The *Passeig de Colom* is Barcelona's sea-front: it skirts the entire area of the port and runs from *Plaça d'Antoni López,* at the far corner of the district of Barceloneta, to the slopes of the hill of Montjuïc. More than 40 metres in width, it is an important thoroughfare where, despite the traffic, it is possible to walk in tranquility. It is one of Barcelona's truly historical sites: one of the many legends narrates that Miguel de Cervantes, the author of *Don Quixote,* lived at n. 33 of *Passeig de Colom* and finished his masterpiece in the Catalan city. His hero too visited Barcelona and was surprized by the sombre, macabre atmosphere of the day. From *Plaça Portal de la Pau,* the *Passeig de Colom* crosses *Plaça del Duc de Medinaceli.* Sombre 19th-century palaces surround this tree-shaded square with its *Monument to Admiral Galceran Marquet* by Daniel Molina. The *Palace of the Capitanía General,* set between the old walls of the convent of the Brothers of Mercy, also lies along *Passeig de Colom.* The long avenue ends in *Plaça d'Antoni López,* adjacent to the lovely *Plaça del Palau.* The *Statue to López* at the centre of the square is by Venancio Vallmitjana. On one side of the square is the large *Post Office Building.*

A view of Plaça del Palau.

The Triumphal Arch, majestic entrance to the Parc de la Ciutadella.

LA CIUTADELLA

Barcellona's large city park, the *Ciutadella*, is a splendid green area covering more than 700 acres: tree-shaded avenues, palms, fields, terraces, statues, gardens, pools and lakes, waterfalls and palaces form a mosaic created according to the classical criteria of late 19th century landscape architecture. The park owes its name to the military fortress Philip V had built here between 1715 and 1718. The Bourbon king, who had won the War of Succession to the throne of Spain, decided to punish Barcelona for having sided with his adversaries. After the conquest of the city, in 1714, the new sovereign dissolved the Catalan parliament, prohibited the Catalan language and razed one of the residential districts, the *Ribera*, to the ground. More than 10,000 inhabitants had lived here and this was where he built the fortified bastions of the *Ciutadella*. In 1808 the French took over the fortification, and it was not until 1869 that the land, on which nothing but ruins then remained, was restored to the city of Barcelona. The idea for a city park took form in those years. The project was by Josep Fontseré with the collaboration of Josep Vilaseca i Casanovas, but it was not until 1888, when the Universal Exhibition was held in the gardens of the *Ciutadella*, that the park acquired its present aspect. The **Triumphal Arch** was built then as the entrance to the Exhibition. It stands 30

A detail of the Triumphal Arch showing the coat of arms in the centre of the impressive frieze by Josep Llimona.

MUSEU D'ART MODERN

Opened in 1945, the Museum of Modern Art is dedicated to Catalan sculpture and painting of the 19th and 20th centuries. Works by the painter Marià Fortuny, from Tarragona are exhibited here together with those of Isidro Nonell, paintings by Josep-Maria Sert as well as Joan Miró, Salvador Dalí (*Portrait of his Father*) and an excellent example of surrealist art by Antoni Tàpies.

SALVADOR DALÍ (1904-1989)

An arrogantly prolific and avantgarde painter and sculptor, motivated by a quest for 'the unusual' and the desire to surprise and provoke, thereby creating polemical discussion, Dali was born in Figueres and remained strongly attached to the city all his life. He studied at Madrid's Academy of Fine Arts, and was susceptible to all the movements from Cubism to Futurism, from the Metaphysical to Surrealism even experimenting with the cinema and literature. With such a complex and controversial personality, he was guaranteed immediate success (his first exhibition was in 1919) that continued to grow to the extent that, by the time he died at Figueres he was considered one of the most interesting artists of the 20th century.

MUSEU DE ZOOLOGIA

The *Zoological Museum* and the *Geological Museum* together consititute the *Ciutadella Museum of Natural Sciences*, dedicated to the natural heritage of Catalonia. The building that houses the museum is known as the 'Castle of the Three Dragons' and was designed by the architect Domènech i Montaner. It was originally the cafè and restaurant of the Universal Exhibition of 1888.

metres high at the end of the *Passeig de Sant Joan* and is a showy structure of moorish inspiration designed and built by Josep Vilaseca. The large tree-shaded avenue leads to the heart of the park. One of the main buildings was originally the old city Arsenal, which, as time went by, was transformed into the Royal Palace and the seat of the **Catalan Parliament**. Today this neoclassic building also houses the Museum of Modern Art. One of the most spectacular attractions of the *Ciutadella* is the fountain known as the *Cascada Monumental*. It was designed by Josep Fontserè, but a young university student still unaware of his great future, by the name of Antoni Gaudí, also contributed to the work. The fountain is decorated with statues by Venanci Vallmitjana, while the *Cuadriga de la Aurora* group on top is by Rosend Nobas (1882). Also of interest are the *Geological Museum* (***Museu Martorell***) with its collections of minerals and palaeontology, and the **Zoological Garden**. Statues are to

be found throughout the park such as a bronze group of *gazelles* by Nuria Tortras and the monument to the *Catalan Volunteers* of World War I. But the most famous statue is the *Senyoreta del paraigu,* an elegant and charming lady shading herself from the sun with a parasol, a work by Roig i Solé (1884) standing above a fountain with two basins and one of the most romantic of the many images of Barcelona.

Above, the fine Cascada Monumental.
Left, the famous 19th century fountain of the Lady with Umbrella.

JOAN ROIG I SOLÉ (1835-1918)

Born in Reus, the same city where Antoni Gaudí was born in 1852, Joan Ruig i Solé was a popular sculptor, particularly renowned for his skill in working marble and the happy creativity that prevades all his works. In official recognition of his art, the city of Barcelona nominated him a member of the Academy of Arts and Sciences. He died in Barcelona in 1918.

MACBA

Over the last few decades Barcelona has devoted particular attention to art and culture as represented by the impressive **MACBA, Barcelona's Museum of Contemporary Art**. Located in *Plaça dels Angels*, this elegant white building was designed and built by Richard Meier and is in itself an attractive example of contemporary art. The result of a joint initiative by the *Museu d'Art Contemporani*,

MUSEU D'ART CONTEM

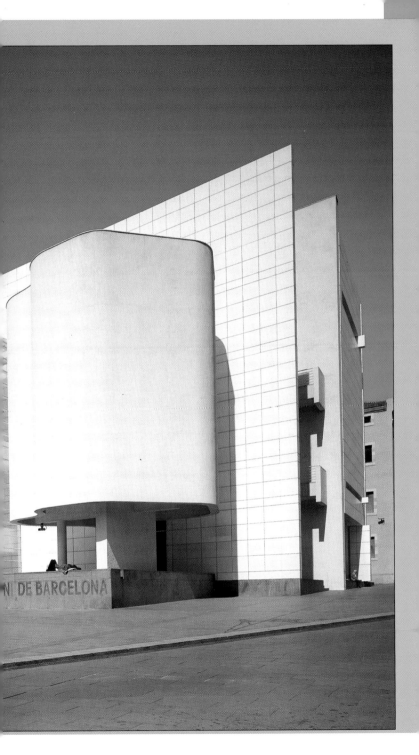

49

The interior of MACBA (Museu d'Art Contemporani) – itself a grandiose, innovative work of art.

Barcelona City Council and the Catalonia Region, the museum was opened in 1995 to provide the city with an Institute that would fill a gap in the area of recent artistic production. The collection is dedicated to international postwar art and has avantgarde works and installations, with an emphasis on Spanish, and in particular Catalan, artists. The permanent collection is continually developing and is housed in specific rooms. Other spaces are dedicated instead to shows and temporary exhibitions. The Museum also runs a lively programme of activities including initiatives of a didactic nature as well as conferences, films and multi-media events.

The Casa de la Caritat, today home to the CCCB and on the right, views of the interior.

CENTRE DE CULTURA CONTEMPORÀNIA

The Centre of Contemporary Culture of Barcelona, or CCCB, is a multi-disciplinary and experimental institution, open to new methods and trends, that organises exhibitions, musical events, ballets, debates, readings and trips to better discover the city of Barcelona. The Centre is specifically dedicated to cities and the new problems (social, urban, cultural) that are inevitably related to their rapid development. Housed in the *Casa de la Caritat*, this historic building situated in the *Raval* area opened its doors to this innovative experience in February 1994 and is a public institution, the positive outcome of a kind of 'consortium' of the *Diputació de Barcelona* and the *Ajuntament de Barcelona*, and is part of the ambitious project to define the new cultural area of Barcelona, strongly supported by the local authorities, with the involvement of all the main city institutions. It is no coincidence that the initials CCCB also represent the three fundamental points of reference of the Centre: "City, Creativity and Culture of Barcelona". The expectation is that this city – a complex urban reality, firmly rooted to its past but also enthusiatically looking to its future – can provide unexpected resources for new artistic creativity, as well as provide an ideal home and perfect laboratory for an on-going exchange of ideas, notions and discoveries that emerge from different experiences drawn from all over the world.

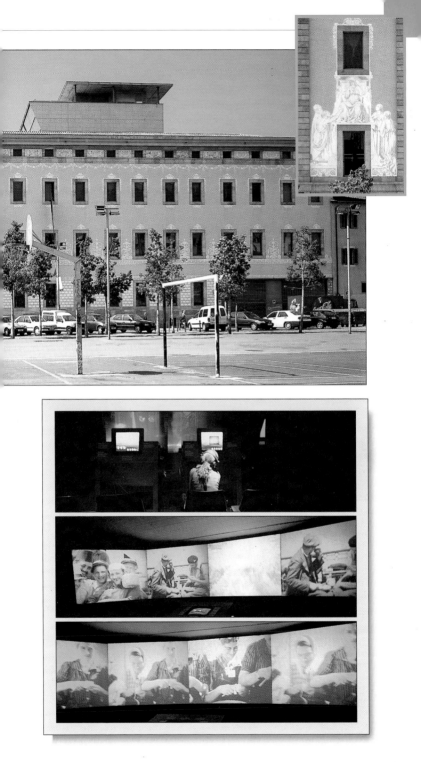

THE WATERFRONT

Three new maritime areas have been created over the last decade as a result of the exceptional project of restoration implemented in the area of Barcelona's port – **Port Vell, Barceloneta** and **Port Olimpic**. The city has thus re-discovered its relationship with the sea and consequently its 5 kilometre-long beach,

spread over three different areas: *Barceloneta*, and the *Sant Sebastià* and *Barceloneta* beaches; the *Vila Olimpica* and the *Nova Icària* and *Bogatell* beaches; *El Poblenou* and the *Mar Bella* and *Nova Mar Bella* beaches. The beaches have also been awarded the European Union's important 'Blue Flag' – recognition not only of the quality of the water and the shores but also of the high standard of the services and infrastructure.

Some typical bars in Barceloneta, yachts moored at the old jetties, modern works of art and avantgarde architecture – the charm of Barcelona's harbour area results from the happy combination of past and present.

FORUM 2004: A GAMBLE FOR THE FUTURE

With the urban reform initiated as part of the Universal Forum of Cultures, 2004, Barcelona has once again shown itself to be one of the liveliest European capitals, able to preserve its own historic Catalan identity while facilitating modernization. At the end of the *Avinguda Diagonal*, the *Parc de Diagonal Mar* has already been opened – an area of 14 hectares of parkland with lakes, fountains and sports grounds. The ambitious **"Diagonal Mar" Project** will cover an area of 34 hectares anad foresees three luxury hotels, a shopping centre with 240 shops, an underground car park for 5,000 vehicles, and several residential areas. At the crossroads between the *Avinguda Diagonal* and the *Calle de Prim*, is the building seen as an emblem of the Forum, by the Swiss architects Herzog and De Meuron, a sort of triangular prism housing conference halls and exhibition space. Linked to the Forum by an underground walkway, the **Centro Internacional de Convenciones**, designed by Josep Lluís Mateo, with a surface area of 68,000 square metres, will be the largest conference centre in Europe. With a design similar to centres in America, the wide horizontal structure will be capable of handling the flow of thousands of people. The project also includes the **Pabellón de la Biodiversidad**, a scientific information centre and a new **Marine Zoo**. The **Explanada del Forum** will cover an area of 150,000 square metres and will be the second largest square in the world after Tienanmen in Beijing.

In the port of Barcelona is the characteristic fishing village of **Barceloneta**, originally created for those who had been evicted to make way for the building of the *Ciutadella.* These attractive little two and three storey houses were built by Juan Martìn de Cermeño in 1753 and the village is famous today mainly for its excellent restaurants, lively local bars and the delightful cafes around the harbour. Still anchored in the port is an active fishing fleet. To see and appreciate the town from a new and unusual viewpoint, you can take a trip on a different type of boat – the **golondrinas**, named 'swift' after the birds. These pleasure craft have special characteristics that enable them to manoeuvre in enclosed areas of water, such as Barcelona's port. Made of wood, their two bridges permit easier navigation in narrow spaces. Very popular with tourists, this fleet of boats

also includes ferries which are larger and more spacious known as 'catamaran-type' *golondrinas.*

The splendour of the port is enhanced by some futuristic buildings such as the **World Trade Center**. Designed by the

BARCELONETA CABLE CAR

You can enjoy an unusual panorama of the city not only from the '*golondrinas*' but also from the *Torre Sant Sebastiá*. Right on the edge of Barceloneta the tower and the cable car that operates from here provide a magnificent view of the entire area of the port. The steel structure, which is 80 metres high, was built at the beginning of the 20th century to connect the two oldest points of the city. The base of the tower is 14.5 metres square and housed at the top are the cable car machinery and the lift, while on the floor

above is a restaurant. With a timetable that varies according to the season, the cable car links Barceloneta to Montjuïc flying over the World Trade Center and stopping on the way at the 'station' of *Torre de Jaume*.

In October 1998 the Barcelona Cable Car Company initiated a difficult process of renovation involving both the tower and the cable cars, still one of the most impressive features of Barcelona's harbour area.

well-known group of architects, Pei Cobb Freed and Partners, the Center stands out against the *Moll* of Barcelona with its profile representing an ocean liner. The building consists of four curved buildings, enclosing a central court of some 2,500 square metres, surrounded by arcades and with a raised central patio enlivened by water-games. Three of the buildings house offices, while the fourth is the *Grand Marina Hotel.*

The futuristic outline of the World Trade Center.

The once neglected and decadent area of **Port Vell** is now one of the many wonders that Barcelona has succeeded in creating over recent years and is part of the vast scheme of urban modernization that began at the time of the 1992 Olympics. Perhaps the greatest rediscovery for the city of Barcelona was its outlet to the sea; despite its location, for years the city had merely felt the presence of the sea, had breathed the sea air, without having fully utilised this vital element. In fact Barcelona was also known as the 'Manchester of Catalonia' as, like the English city, it too had developed towards the interior, with its back turned to the sea. Today *Port Vell* covers over 55 hectares and is a lively and integral part of the city with many cultural, sporting and recreational facilities. Close to the beautiful Gothic buildings, and to the masterpieces of Gaudí and Picasso, the modern sports complexes in the *Marina Port Vell* attract thousands of visitors and lovers of the sea every year. Without doubt the most popular and interesting centre in *Port Vell* is the **Maremagnum**, an elegant translucent building with pure horizontal lines designed by Helio Pinon, Albert Viaplana, Rafael Coll and Ricard Mercadé. Open every day of the year, this large shopping centre has shops, restaurants, and a cinema complex. Beside the Maremagnum is the **Rambla de Mar**, a suspension bridge with an unusual curved outline that links the *Moll d'Espanya* to the *Moll de la Fusta*. Also designed by Pinon and Viaplana, it was opened in September 1994 and is the perfect continuation of the larger and older *Rambla*, perhaps representing Barcelona's return towards the sea that it had for so long ignored.

Some of the many futuristic structures that now characterise and enhance the architecture of the Port Vell area: the Maremagnum housing several cinemas and the Rambla de Mar.

Also in *Port Vell* is the **Aquarium**, the largest in Europe and the most important in the world for the Mediterranean sea. The Aquarium is divided into various sections representing all the various marine habitats of the world (8,000 forms of life divided into 300 species) but its greatest attraction is the 80 metre long glass tunnel which submerges the visitor in the silent, magical world of the ocean.

With its modern design and bright colours the Aquarium is one of the main attractions of Port Vell.

SHARKS

These impressive carnivorous animals can submerge to 70 metres depth and generally inspire fear and hatred. This is probably because, attracted and excited by the vibrations of a wounded fish, they hasten to the scene of a hunt where an animal may be speared and thrash in the water losing blood. They therefore clash violently with the divers who are hunting the fish. The frequent and merciless meetings between shark and diver have therefore created the image of the shark as an implacable and blood-thirsty predator. However, since sharks have been chased away from most tropical resorts, it has often been noted that their attitude has completely changed: diffident and shy, they are not easily approached and will escape immediately at the least sign of pursuit by man. It is therefore interesting to observe them from the glass tunnel of the aquarium, external to, yet immerged in their own environment, where one can appreciate aspects that have been ignored previously. Seeing the sharks below water it is fascinating to note their sinuosity, their elegant and powerful way of moving and behaving like true aristocrats of the sea. This is only one of the amazing possibilities offered by the Aquarium and its futuristic structure.

Grey shark (Carcharhinus amblyrhynchos).

IMAX PORT VELL

A revolutionary cinema complex, the *Imax Port Vell* boasts three different projection systems: Imax, Omnimax and 3D. The first system projects the film onto a flat screen 21 metres high, the equivalent of a 7-storey building, with a surface area of 600 square metres. The Omnimax system projects onto a hemispherical screen that 'wraps around' the viewer, who is thus emersed in the action. Lastly, the 3D system is used with polarized glasses, high-technology projectors and an Imax screen. And all of this is matched by a 27,000 watt powered digital sound system.

MUSEU D'HISTÒRIA DE CATALUNYA

The *Museum of the History of Catalonia* is housed in an important example of port-architecture (the old General Warehouses of the Port of Barcelona, refurbished in 1901 by the engineer and architect Elies Rogent) and is fundamental to an understanding of the tradition and culture of the country, offering a fascinating interactive trip through the history of Catalonia. Eight sections are organised chronologically, from pre-history to the present day: 'Early Times'; 'the Birth of a Nation'; 'Our Sea'; 'To the Ends of the Empire'; 'The Foundations of the Industrial Revolution'; 'Steam and Nation'; 'The Electric Era'; 'Decline and Rebirth'. The Museum has an extensive media library and ably combines general and more technical information with skillful use of drawings, historical reconstructions, objects and audiovisual documentation.

Below, two views of the old General Warehouses, now housing the Museu d'Història de Catalunya.

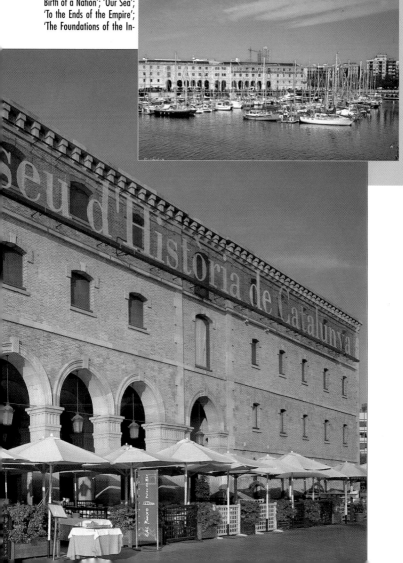

The two tower blocks on the *Carrer de la Marina*, commonly referred to as the 'Twin Towers' provide a monumental entrance to the area of the **Port Olimpic**. The **Mapfre Tower** is a 43-floor office block, 154 metres high, and was built in 1992 by the architects Inigo Ortiz and Enrique Leòn. Also 154 metres high, the second tower block houses the **Hotel Arts**, and is built in 'Structural Expressionist' style (also known as 'high tech modernism').

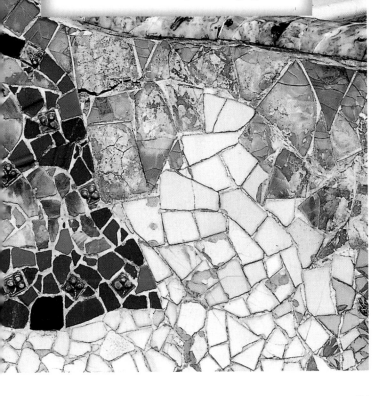

ANTONI GAUDÍ AND MODERNISM

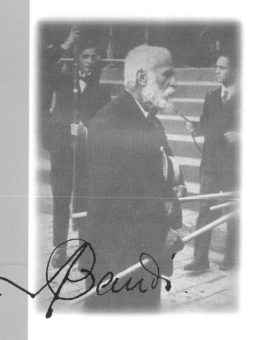

on the urban structure of Barcelona. Casa Vicens, one of his works dated between 1878 and 1888, Casa Güell built 1885-90 and named after the man who commissioned it, the wealthy industrialist and art patron Eusebi Güell, the Colegio de Santa Teresa de Jesús, 1889-94, all testify to his eclectic interweaving of experimental forms that were modern in style with elements of local tradition.

In the 1890s he accentuated his tendency to make inventive use of colour and imaginative sculptural decoration, while maintaining the evident references to Catalan culture. One example is the repeated use in Parc Güell of dragons, figures which played an important part in the legends of Catalonia. Included in the wealth of daring ornamentation, sometimes reaching the limits of artistic delirium, are forms inspired by the vitality of nature, especially in the 20th-century works, such as Casa Milà, whose undulating architecture echoes the multiform aspects of the sea, and, naturally, his unfinished masterpiece, the Sagrada Familia.

Gaudí took over the project for this new building in 1884. During almost forty years of work he conceived an architectural plan which united all the elements of his art. Of the three façades planned, he saw only the first - the Nativity - completed, for he died in Barcelona in 1926. His remains are in the crypt of the Sagrada Familia, whose lofty bell towers leave the imprint of his style in the heart of Barcelona. In 1957 Le Corbusier defined him as "the builder of the 1900s" and modern critics have acknowledged his capacity to unite the skills of builder, sculptor, painter and architect, whether of substantial structures or interiors, large as well as small.

Antoni Gaudí was born in Reus, near Barcelona, on June 25, 1852. The son of an ironsmith, he first studied in his native town, but from 1876 he continued his cultural studies in Barcelona where he attended the school of architecture, graduating in 1878.

The architectural restoration that the famous French architect Viollet-Le Duc was carrying out on the walls of Carcassonne at the time, strongly influenced Gaudí. In these early years, in which he probably created the four winged dragons in the Park of the Ciutadella, Gaudí developed his original architectural aesthetic. Inspired by both the Spanish national form of Gothic art and elements peculiar to the Catalan culture, he then gradually absorbed and integrated the stylistic features of art nouveau, the new artistic-cultural movement which permeated much of European artistic expression at the end of the 19th century. By around 1880 he was already able to share a dominant role in Catalan Modernism with Domènech i Montaner.

Between the 1880s and 90s, he created a series of works which left an indelible mark

SAGRADA FAMILIA

The unfinished church that represents Gaudí's life's work.
Open from November to February: 9-18 – September,
October and March: 9-19 – April to August: 9-20.
Closed 25 and 26 December; 1 and 6 January.

PARC GÜELL

Gaudí's most colourful masterpiece, proclaimed a World
Heritage Site by UNESCO.
Open: March to October: 10-19 – April and September: 10-20
– May to August: 10-21 – November to February: 10-18.

CASA MILÀ

The house with the
bizarre chimneys.
Open every day, 10-20.

CASA BATLLÓ

Passeig de Gracia 43
Visit at request.

PALAU GÜELL

Designed by
Gaudí for the
Güell family.
Open from
Monday to Friday:
10-14 and 16-
19.30.

CASA VICENS

A splendid fantasy of colours and decoration.
Not open to the public.

CASA CALVET

The roughness of the stone contrasts with the refined
decorations. Not open to the public.

BELLESGUARD

The *modernista*
castle with Gothic
features.
Usually not open
to the public.

CONVENT OF
SANTA TERESA

Sombre gothic-
modernista building.
Visits by appointment
every Saturday
from 11am.

FINCA
MIRALLES

Wall and
gateway that
are pure
fantasy.

GÜELL
PAVILIONS
(PEDRALBES)

Magnificent
fantasy creations
at the summer
residence of the
Güell family.

STREET
LAMPS

Energy and
magic in the
centre of
Plaça Reial.

Sagrada Familia

Gaudí's intense series of works culminates in what is considered his masterpiece, even though it was left incomplete at his sudden death – the *Sagrada Familia*.

In 1866, a book dealer named Bocabella founded a spiritual association dedicated to St. Joseph. In 1881 two hectares of land in the Barrio del Poblet, a modest district in the outskirts of the city, were acquired with the contributions of a public subscription. Initially the construction of a church dedicated to the Holy Family was entrusted to the architects Martorell and Francesc de Paula de Villar. After having begun the construction of the crypt, the latter resigned and Martorell called on Gaudí, then aged 31. On the death of the bookseller Bocabella, the Bishop of Barcelona officially took over what had been a private initiative and formally put Gaudí in charge of the works. He had, at the time, already finished the vault of the crypt and radically changed Villar's original plan. Gaudí saw the *Sagrada Familia* as a great symbolic building, a colossal allegory of the life of Christ, to be represented in three monumental *façades*. The west façade was to be dedicated to the *Nativity*, the one on the east to the *Passion* and the façade to the south to the *Ascension*. So perfect and complete is the *Nativity Façade* that it can be considered as a building in its own right. The three portals, which symbolize *Faith, Hope*, and *Charity*, are completely covered with sculpture in art nouveau style, and the architecture disappears under a forest of vibrant figures which stretch, twist, and expand. The *portal of Hope*, dedicated to the Virgin, shows the mystical *Marriage of Mary and Joseph*, the *Flight into Egypt* and the *Massacre of the Innocents*. The palm-shaped column is supported by a Nile tortoise, symbol of perseverance. The central *portal of Charity* is divided by the *tree of descendants from Abraham to Joseph* and is dominated by the *grotto of Bethlehem*. The cypress tree is crowned by a *Tau Cross* and features a pelican, symbol of sacrifice, at its base. The last portal, on the right, is dedi-

Sagrada Familia

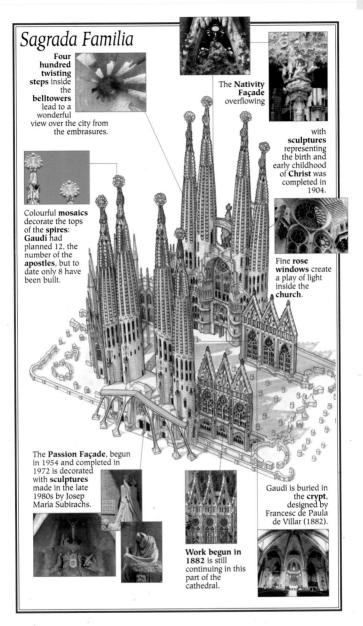

Four hundred twisting steps inside the **belltowers** lead to a wonderful view over the city from the embrasures.

The **Nativity Façade** overflowing

with **sculptures** representing the birth and early childhood of **Christ** was completed in 1904.

Colourful **mosaics** decorate the tops of the **spires**: **Gaudí** had planned 12, the number of the **apostles**, but to date only 8 have been built.

Fine **rose windows** create a play of light inside the **church**.

The **Passion Façade**, begun in 1954 and completed in 1972 is decorated with **sculptures** made in the late 1980s by Josep María Subirachs.

Gaudí is buried in the **crypt**, designed by Francesc de Paula de Villar (1882).

Work begun in 1882 is still continuing in this part of the cathedral.

cated to St. Joseph and illustrates stories of *Jesus in the Temple and in the carpenter's workshop.*

A look at Gaudí's working methods throws some light on the composition of the allegoric representations. The master

Following pages: two spectacular views of the Passion Façade and the Nativity Façade, the only one that Gaudí was able to bring to completion.

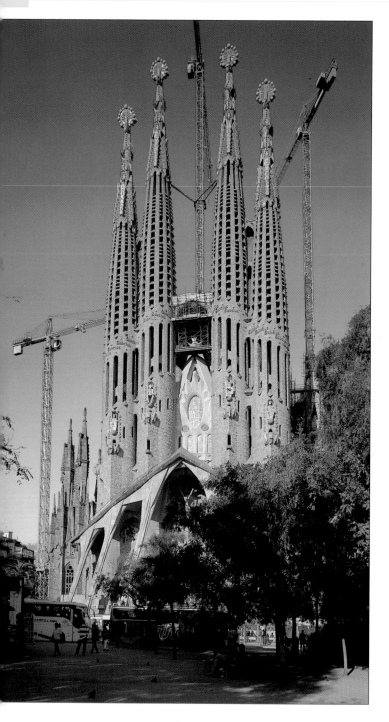

used to choose his models from people in the street, then photograph them against a group of mirrors so as to have a complete view from all angles. After that he made a plaster cast which he then used for the figure, modifying the proportions as he saw fit. The models preserved in the crypt show Barcelona's "unfinished cathedral" as a traditional Latin cross plan with five aisles meeting in a transept of three. The nave is illuminated by wide windows and was to be a real forest of columns,

each dedicated to a saint, an apostle, or a bishop. At the crossing of the transept, a colossal central tower, a symbol of Christ, was to rise up surrounded by four smaller towers (symbols of the Four *Evangelists*). Each of the three façades was to have four bell towers, making a total of twelve, to symbolize the *Apostles.*

As is evident from the model which Gaudí presented at the 1910 Paris Exhibition, the church was to be further decorated by brilliant colours. On the Nativity Façade, the portal of Hope was to have been green, symbolizing the valley of the Nile. The portal of Charity was to be the blue of a night in Bethlehem and the portal of Faith was to have been burnt Sienna to symbolize the sands of Palestine. The interior of the church was also to have been coloured: white and gold in the right aisle to symbolize joy, violet and black in the left side aisle to symbolize grief.

Gaudí threw himself heart and soul into this colossal work. In 1914 when he was already 62 he even decided to live in a

Left, a detail of the mosaic decoration of one of the remarkable spires with two belltowers. Right, the splendid Passion Façade, by Josep María Subirachs with some most expressive sculptures.

room in the building yard of the church. When he died, the work was carried on, according to his plans, by a group of his closest collaborators including Sugranes, Quintana and Matamela. Work was interrupted in 1935 when the Spanish Civil War broke out, during which time a fire destroyed part of the building and many plans and models in Gaudí's studio. Still today, financed by the contributions of

More details of the amazing sculptural decoration of the Sagrada Familia: shown here are some groups in art nouveau style on the Nativity Façade.

Located in the crypt, the *Museum of the Sagrada Familia* contains about 20 original designs by Gaudí, all that remains following the fire of 1935. There are also drawings, plans, models, photos of the various phases of construction and audiovisuals. The visitor can imagine how Gaudí's dream will look when finally finished. And perhaps also make a contribution to it.

Two models of how the church should finally appear.

the faithful, construction continues, albeit extremely slowly. When it is finished, the *Sagrada Familia* should be 110 metres long and 45 high – one of the largest and finest churches in the Christian world. The **Museum of the Sagrada Familia** is part of the complex: wall panels, showcases and photographs have been

Rose window and other architectural elements of highly original design and below right, the tranquil crypt where Gaudí is buried.

arranged in some of the rooms. An interesting documentary survey in chronological order makes it possible to follow the various building phases of what has been terminated so far of the ambitious project drawn up by Gaudí.

THE SAGRADA FAMILIA TODAY

Gaudí was fond of saying that the Sagrada Familia was an 'on-going job' and when asked when it would be finished he would reply, "The client who commissioned this church is in no hurry." In fact this immense incomplete structure has always been an open site, and the continuing work, financed by numerous donations, is based on the sketches made by Gaudí's pupils and collaborators as many of his original plans were destroyed during the Civil War. Even today Barcelona is divided between two schools of thought: those who would like to see the church finally completed, and those who would leave it as it is.

Güell Park

Beginning work in 1900, with Eusebi Güell as his patron once more, Gaudí created one of his loveliest works, the *Parc Güell*. The genius and art of the Spanish architect could never have been expressed fully without the presence in Barcelona of his patron, Eusebi Güell i Bacigalupi. The wealthy count of Güell, who greatly admired the English garden-cities so fashionable at the time, wanted to create a residential district of about 60 homes on 15 hectares of land he owned in an area called "Montaña Pelada". The inhabitants were promised a radically new way of life. Gaudí was commissioned to prepare an ideal town plan, with complete freedom of expression as far as buildings and decoration were concerned. Despite the most optimistic previsions, the experiment of the new garden-city failed. Only two of the 60 plots were sold, one to Gaudí himself and the other to a friend, Dr. Alfonso Trias. Consequently, in 1922 the City of Barcelona acquired the entire area and transformed it into a public park. A high wall encloses the area and the main entrance is at

Some of the most colourful creations of the explosive Gaudí: the Güell Park that UNESCO has declared a World Heritage site; above, the sinuous twin stairway which leads to the Room of One Hundred Columns; below, one of the typical zoomorphical figures that decorate it gleaming with lively mosaic work, as too are many other decorative elements dotted around the park.

the intersection with *Carrer d'Olot*. The two curious pavilions with polychrome tiles which flank the splendid wrought-iron gate were originally meant to serve as a porter's lodge (on the right) and as an administrative office

(on the left). A double staircase departs from the entrance and the flights of stairs, with ornamental waterworks and zoomorphic sculptures covered with mosaics (including the dragons always present in Gaudí's art), meet at the top in what is commonly called the "Room of One Hundred Columns", though there are only 86. In this capricious "hypostyle hall" the Doric columns bend to support a vault which also seems to be moving because it is wavy, and, in a surprising anticipation of Pop Art, encrusted with pieces of bottles, plates, glass and ceramics.

In 1912 Gaudí put the crowning touch on this hall in what is considered the symbol and synthesis of his "total art" - the great curved bench which marks the edge of the upper terrace overlooking the city. It is said that in his attempt to give the surface of the bench an anatomical form, Gaudí had one of his workers sit

nude on wet plaster and thus obtained the profile which he then used in designing the seat. Here too, Gaudí is once more a skilled forerunner of the form and colour of an art form which did not yet exist: in fact the entire bench is composed of a mosaic of ceramic shards of various colours and sizes which he arranged in a gigantic abstract collage. At the centre of the park is **Gaudí's** unusual **House-Museum**, where he lived from 1906 to 1926 and which still preserves the furniture, paintings, and objects which belonged to this great Catalan artist.

Above left, the large terrace above the Room of One Hundred Columns and, below, a detail of the famous undulating bench that circles the room, believed to be the longest in the world. Above and right, further examples of Gaudí's versatility in creating decorative structures and elements.

85

Casa Milà

Casa Milà, begun in 1905 and finished five years later, is situated on *Passeig de Gracia*. A glance at the façade suffices to explain why this five-story building is better known as *"La Pedrera"* or the quarry. The *Pedrera* may very well be the best and most complete example of Gaudí's concept of Nature: a sort of stone mountain created by man, a group of "caverns" opening onto the façade from which emanates an enormous vital force.

Gaudí, this solitary introvert and fervent Catholic, succeeded here in transforming the most fundamental concepts of art nouveau into an expression of pure vitality: something that is no longer a static geometric space, but a space which expands with its creation and development. The façade thus materializes in a series of waves which follow the movement of the entire building. Indeed, Gaudí himself once said: "...corners will disappear and the material will abundantly manifest itself in its astral rotundities: the sun will penetrate on all four sides and it will be the image of paradise... and my palace will be more luminous than light."

But let us climb for a moment to the roof of the house, and receive the full impact of the unrestrained fantasy of the artist. No railings, but gardens overlooking deep courtyards, with hooded

The spectacular sinuous façade of Casa Milà with elaborate wrought iron balconies and gigantic chimneys.

Two internal views of Casa Milà: above, the attic with a display on the works of Gaudí and below a carefully reconstructed dining room of a well-to-do family.

Following pages, views of the roof terrace of Casa Milà with the bizarre, almost ghostly figures of the incredible chimneys.

monsters of enigmatic and disquieting aspect. In this abstract theatrical scene (even the shapes of the chimneys are bizarre) Gaudí anticipates by a good forty years aspects of pure Surrealism.

ESPAI GAUDÍ. EL PIS DE LA PEDRERA

In 1986 a Catalan bank, the Caixa de Catalunya, bought *Casa Milà*, which was falling into a slow but steady state of disrepair, with the intention of restoring it and converting it into a cultural centre for the city. Ten years of careful and intelligent repair returned *Casa Milà* to its original splendour and it became the Cultural Foundation of the Caixa de Catalunya, a permanent exhibition for the appreciation of Gaudí's art. The *Espai Gaudí*, dedicated to a deeper understanding of the master's architecture, fully documents, his work, presenting it within a historical and biographical context. The central part of the exhibition is dedicated to presenting and explaining Gaudí's contribution to 20th century architecture including a series of models that illustrate the basic concepts of his art. On the fourth floor is *El Pis de la Pedrera*, an area of 569 square metres where the appartment of a bourgeoise family of the early 20th century is reconstructed. Each room has maintained its original purpose. Lastly is the terrace of the *Pedrera* which has remained as it was in 1912. The view from atop, among the fantastic chimneys and bizarre domes offers a breathtaking sweep over the monuments of Barcelona.

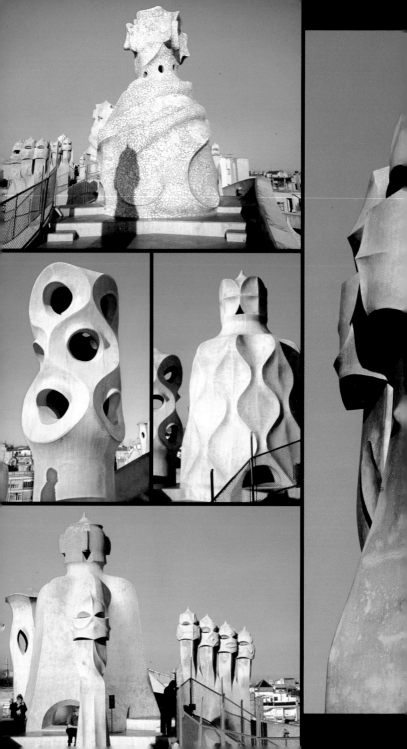

Casa Batlló

Casa Batlló, at no. 43 *Passeig de Gracia*, was built between 1904 and 1906 in the city block known as the *"Manzana de la Discòrdia"* or the "Apple of Discord", after the strange and diverse examples of Catalan *modernista* (art nouveau) architecture seen here. *Casa Batlló* was restored by Gaudí for the family of José Batlló i Casanovas. Gaudí applied his own extremely personal style to the whole building, restructuring the façade, restoring the interior and redesigning the furniture. An "immense, crazy, multicoloured mosaic shimmering with scintillating light from which forms of water appear" is how Salvador Dalí described *Casa Batlló*. The cult of

the curved line and the expansion of the form as a pure and vital symbol reach their apex here: everything, from the columns to the balconies and the unique roof covered with tiles laid like scales, is seen as something that must be made to vibrate and live.

Palau Güell

Between 1885 and 1890, Gaudí built this palace on the *Carrer Nou de la Rambla* for Eusebi Güell, the cotton magnate who had 'discovered' his work at the Paris International Exhibition in 1878. Here, for the first time, Gaudí introduced the play on

space on the roof, covering the chimneys and ventilation outlets with shards of ceramics, and arranging them around a central cone which corresponded to the internal skylight through which light penetrated and was diffused inwards.

The interior is a magnificent synthesis of ivory and marble, carved wood, patterned glass and gilded metals.

Above, the façade of Casa Batlló.

Views of Palau Güell, with the lofty chimneys completely covered with coloured ceramic fragments.

Casa Vicens

The villa located at 24 *Carrer de les Carolines* is the result of the commission given to the young and inexperienced Gaudí in 1878 by the entrepreneur Vicens. The building, begun in 1883 and completed in 1888, was a brilliant debut for the young architect, as this was one of his first works. The façade demonstrates a balanced combination of elements which, with their play of geometric forms, recall Islamic architecture, while the colour of the ceramic decoration stands out against the rough texture of the natural stone and brick. Despite the simplicity of the materials employed, the overall impression is unexpectedly beautiful. When enlargements were carried out in 1925-26, some of the magnificent gardens which surrounded the villa were lost. Of particular note are the wrought-iron railings, where palm leaves provide the basic decorative motif. Continuing to apply his unbridled fantasy, the equally fascinating interior of the house was also planned and designed by Gaudí.

Casa Calvet

The house which now stands at 48 Calle de Casp was completed between 1898 and 1899. The building is adorned with a wealth of decorative detail: the façade, built of great blocks of stone, is enlivened by numerous balconies with wrought-iron railings, while at the top are two elegant curved pediments. The lower floors of the building were to be used as shops and offices while the upper floors were to serve as dwellings. Gaudí not only planned the outside of the house, but also designed the furniture which is still on display inside.

Top, two views of Casa Vicens where the rough stone contrasts with the elegant decorations and, left, two details of Casa Calvet showing the sophisticated decoration.

Bellesguard

In 1900 Doña Maria Sagués commissioned Gaudí to build a country house that was to reaffirm the historical and symbolic meaning of its particular location, for it was here that the last king of Aragon, Martin I, had a country house called *Bell Esguard* built in 1408, a name inspired by the truly magnificent panorama of the city to be had from here. The entire building was therefore intended to recall one of the most felicitous periods in Catalan history - a sort of medieval dream, or ode to antiquity. Antoni Gaudí, "the most Catalan of the Catalonians" as his friend Joquim Torres defined him, created a relatively simple plan almost perfectly square, onto which he grafted neo-Gothic elements of great elegance: the magnificent portal, protected by a highly decorated wrought-iron grill, the crenellation and the slender spire. The building remained incomplete however and was terminated by Domènec Sugranes in 1917.

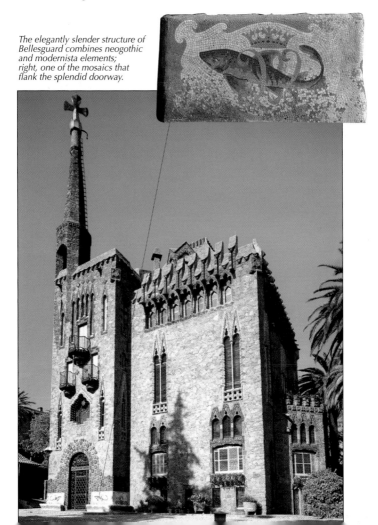

The elegantly slender structure of Bellesguard combines neogothic and modernista elements; right, one of the mosaics that flank the splendid doorway.

The Convent of Santa Teresa

Situated at 85 *Carrer de Ganduxer*, the convent belongs to the first phase of Gaudí's career. The nuns who live there and teach in the college housed in the convent belong to the Order of Saint Teresa of Ávila. The philosophy of this order, based on poverty and parsimony, was kept in mind by the architect and dominates the entire building, which is, in effect, lacking in ornamental detail.

Instead, Gaudí gave the complex a sculptural value resulting almost exclusively from the structure itself. The work is characterised by this concept and by the steeply curved brick arches and iron grill at the entrance. Despite the unquestionable Gothic influence imposed by the nature of the Order and Gaudí's own interest in the Gothic, it is, however, considered an example of 'Modernisme' (art nouveau).

The sombre and austere Convent of Santa Teresa where Gothic-style elements blend perfectly with the structures of the modernista building.

Miralles Estate (Finca)

In 1901 the publisher Hermengild Miralles asked his friend Gaudí to design a wall to completely enclose the property he owned in Sarrià. Gaudí linked 36 separate sections together to create an unusual sinuous, undulating wall. All that now remains of this art nouveau masterpiece is the exceptional gate where a bronze statue of Gaudí himself has recently been placed.

Güell Estate (Finca)

In 1884 Eusebi Güell commissioned Gaudí to design two pavilions for his summer residence at Pedralbes (the Güell estate) in the outskirts of the city. The two pavilions – one octagonal and the other rectangular – are linked by a wrought iron gate shaped like a dragon, a symbolic evocation of the labours of Hercules, mythical founder of Barcelona, in the Garden of the Hesperides. This work was probably greatly influenced by Gaudí's acquaintance with Jacint Verdaguer, the foremost poet of Catalonia's *Renaixença* and the author of the epic poem *Atlantida*. On either side of the gate are the lodge and the stables – a splendid circular building decorated with multi-coloured ceramic fragments.

The street lamps of Plaça Reial

The matter of street lighting was very important in *modernista* Barcelona and some interesting structures were created. For example, as part of a competition for urban lighting, organised by the city council in 1878, Gaudí created the impressive stone and bronze lamps in the Plaça Reial. Believing that it was important the lamps should last for a long time, he chose materials that would resist erosion caused by the weather.

Above, the statue of Gaudí and the entrance to what was once the Miralles Estate; centre, the magnificent wrought iron gate of Pedralbes; right, one of the fine street lamps that Gaudí designed for Plaça Reial.

Born in Barcelona in 1850, Lluís Domènech i Montaner was not only a builder of houses and palaces. He was fascinated by mineralogy, botany and zoology and at first he studied physics and natural sciences before changing direction definitively in favour of architecture. An excellent designer and writer, he defined his own concept of modern architecture, which also succeeded in expressing the nationalistic Catalonian character, in an article entitled En busca d'una arquitectura nacional (In Search of a National Architecture), published in the journal "La Renaixença". His style is entirely original and combines the sinuous lines of art nouveau with the rich ornamentation of hispano-arabic architecture. His practice of combining different materials such as ceramics with iron, or decorated glass, gave rise to unusual results as can be seen in the Palace of Catalonian Music, dated 1908. Montaner died in Barcelona in 1923.

Josep Puig i Cadafalch was an architect, historian and politician. Born in Mataró in 1867, he later moved to Barcelona and in 1895 received his first important commission – Casa Martí. Considered to be the last representative of art nouveau, Cadafalch had three different stylistic phases. The first was inspired by traditional aristocratic Catalan architecture and is evident in buildings such as Casa Martí, Casa Macaya, Casa Amatller and especially Casa de les Punxes (1905). In his second phase Cadafalch interpreted the styles requested by the new bourgeoisie, with the more rational forms seen in the Casa Trinxet and the Casa Company. His third phase, developed at the time of the Universal Exhibition in Barcelona in 1929, was more monumental and is characterised by imposing baroque structures inspired by Roman architecture. On 14 May 1917 he also took on a poltical role, becoming a member of the Permanent Council of the Mancomunitat, the body that eventually became today's Generalitat de Catalunya. In November 1917, after the death of Enric Prat de la Riba, he was elected president of the Generalitat and in 1921 and 1923 was re-elected. The author of numerous studies on Catalonian architecture, from 1942 unitl his death in 1957 he was president of the Insitute of Catalonian Studies.

M O D E R N

THE DECORATIVE STYLE KNOWN AS LIBERTY IN ENGLAND AND ART NOUVEAU IN FRANCE, WAS KNOWN AS *MODERNISTA* IN CATALONIA. HERE, AS IN OTHER COUNTRIES, THE MOVEMENT RESULTED FROM A DESIRE FOR RENEWAL AND IN OPPOSITION TO THE REIGNING BOURGEOIS TASTE IN ART.

THERE CAN BE NO QUESTION THAT WITHOUT THE PRESENCE OF THE MILLIONAIRE EUSEBI GÜELL I BACIGALUPI IN BARCELONA ANTONI GAUDÍ WOULD NOT HAVE BEEN ABLE TO FULLY EXPRESS HIS GENIUS. BUT AROUND THE CENTRAL CHARACTER OF THIS UNUSUAL MAN, SO SOLITARY, SO VERY RELIGIOUS AND SO ISOLATED FROM THE REST OF THE ART WORLD, WERE SEVERAL OTHER PERSONALITIES WHO HELPED TRANSFORM THE FACE OF BARCELONA. DURING THE PERIOD OF THE CATALONIAN "*RENAIXENÇA*" ARCHITECTS SUCH AS LLUÍS DOMÈNECH I MONTANER, FRANCES BERENGUER, MARTORELL, JOAN RUBIÓ I BELIVER, JOSEP PUIG I CADAFALCH, GRANELL ETC., MADE A NAME FOR THEMSELVES WITH WORKS SUCH AS THE *CASA AMATLLER*, OR *CASA ROVIRALTA*, OR THE PALACE OF CATALAN MUSIC.

AT THE CLOSE OF THE 19TH CENTURY BARCELONA BEGAN TO CHANGE AND TOOK ON A NEW IDENTITY. NOT ONLY WERE THE BUILDINGS THEMSELVES SUDDENLY ANIMATED WITH SURPRISING ZOOMORPHIC FEATURES (AN OUTSTANDING EXAMPLE IS THE INCREDIBILE "BUTTERFLY HOUSE" OF *CALLE LLANSA*), BUT THE VARIOUS ACCESSORIES OF STREET FURNITURE WERE ALSO PART OF THIS TRANSFORMATION: STREETS AND AVENUES WERE DECORATED WITH WROUGHT IRON LAMPS, THE GATEWAYS OF ESTATES WERE ENRICHED WITH VOLUTES AND CURLICUES, THE LIGHTNING RODS ON THE ROOFS TWISTED INTO FANTASTIC SHAPES, THE BALCONIES AND RAILINGS SEEMED TO SWELL, CRUMPLE, BEND UNDER AN INVISIBLE HAND. IT IS ALSO THESE ANONYMOUS CRAFTSMEN WHO GAVE BARCELONA THAT REFINED AND ELEGANT ASPECT WHICH DISTINGUISHES IT IN THE PANORAMA OF SPANISH ART.

I S T   A R T

Casa Lleó Morera

Located on *Passeig de Gracia*, close to *Casa Batlló*, this phantasmagorical residence was restructured between 1902 and 1906 by Domènech i Montaner who gave full leash to his fantasy on the façade covering it with sculptures and ornamental friezes. On the level of the second floor statues of four women represent *Progress,* each holding in her hand an invention of this new century: a light bulb, a gramophone, a camera and a telephone. Inside the house, the dining room is magnificent and airy, one of the most beautiful in all Barcelona, lit by coloured glass designed by Lluis Rigalt and decorated with lively panels of mosaic ceramics by Gaspar Homar.

Details of the façade and tower of Casa Lleó Morera. Domènech i Montaner gave full rein to his creative fantasy in the decorative scheme.

The elegant building that houses the Fundació Tàpies, crowned by an original aerial sculpture in anodized aluminium.

The Montaner i Simón Publishing House

Built by Lluís Domènech i Montaner between 1880 and 1885 in *Carrer d'Aragó* in the *Eixample* district - the heart of Barcelona's *modernista* area - and decorated with elements drawn from Islamic architecture, the building was originally the main office of the publisher Montaner i Simón. The busts and names of literary figures sculpted at the top of the façade symbolically recall the original function.

The building was subsequently restored and became home to the Antoni Tàpies Foundation. A work by the artist, *Nùvol i Cadira*, tops the space between the two buildings on high. This outstanding sculpture is made of 2,700 metres of anodized aluminium that twists, turns and bends into curves and spirals forming a gigantic abstract design in the air.

ANTONI TÀPIES FOUNDATION

The Antoni Tàpies Foundation was created in 1984 by the Catalan artist himself, after buying the building, by now almost in ruins, and commissioning Roser Amadò and Lluís Domènech Girbau to restore it. His main aim was to promote knowledge of modern art and culture. The Foundation houses a permanent collection of Tàpies' work as well as temporary exhibitions of modern artists. A specialised library and continual collaboration with internationally famous artists contribute to achieving the aims of this great artist.

ANTONI TÀPIES

Antoni Tàpies, the greatest living Catalan artist, was born in Barcelona on 13 December 1923. His father was a lawyer and his mother came from a family of booksellers and Catalan nationalist politicians who were actively involved in the events of the day. Tàpies grew up in a highly tolerant cultural atmosphere, vibrant with new ideas and creativity, in contact with important public figures who were friends of his father. Following school in Barcelona, he came into contact with the world of contemporary art and, through the journal "D'Aci i d'Allà" edited by Josep Lluís Sert and Joan Prats, he discovered the works of famous artists such as Picasso, Braque, Mondrian, Brancusi, Kandinsky, Duchamp, Klee and Miró. Tàpies was strongly influenced by the latter two but it was the work of Jean Dubuffet that converted him to the abstract and lead him to produce paintings with raw materials while also making collages with waste material. He has received many awards and prizes over the years: the Medaille d'Or for the artistic and moral value of his work in 1966 in Menton; the Fine Arts Gold Medal from the Spanish government in 1981; the national Grand Prix for painting from the French government; honorary member of the Royal Academy of Arts, London in 1992. Numerous retrospective exhibitions are held throughout the world, always with great critical and public success.

Hospital de Sant Pau

The original austere nucleus of the *Hospital de Sant Pau* (Saint Paul's Hospital), which today covers an extensive area and is one of the finest examples of Catalan *Modernisme,* was the *Hospital de la Santa Creu* (Holy Cross) dating from 1401. By the end of the 19th century, however, it had become too small for the number of patients and it was extended. Work began in 1902 thanks to the decisive contribution of the banker Pau Gil, and the task was awarded to the architect Lluís Domènech i Montaner. Numerous artists collaborated in the decoration of the new building including the sculptors Eusebi Arnau i Mascort, who made the emblem of the hospital, and Pau Gargallo i Catalàn who made the beautiful statues representing the *Theological Virtues.* The innovative design of the hospital complex, named for the donor's onomastic saint, is accentuated by the wealth of coloured ceramic decoration.

The Palace of Catalan Music

Declared a World Heritage Site in 1987 by UNESCO, this building is one of the masterpieces of the *modernista* architect Lluís Domènech i Montaner. The palace was opened in 1908 not far from *Plaça de Catalunya* and houses the prestigious institute of music 'Orfeó Català' founded in 1891 by Lluís Millet and Amadeu Vives who were responsible for recording and conserving traditional Catalan music and songs. The red brick façade is decorated with mosaics by Lluís Bru and an attractive sculpture representing *Popular Music* by Miquel Blay. The interior is a feast of decorative glass, mosaics and sculptures in pure *modernista* style – such as the *Winged Horse* by Eusebi Arnau, or the statues of the *Muses* in the hemicycle, and especially the magnificent *Concert Hall* a glittering casket of coloured glass dominated by the skylight in the centre designed by Rigalt and Granel. The palace's history reflects the history of music in the 20th century. The greatest musicians have all performed here: on 15 May 1908 Richard Strauss directed the famous Berlin Philarmonic Orchestra, and in the same year Pablo Casals held his first concert here. In 1961 Rubenstein performed in the palace and in 1921 Albert Schweitzer played the organ in *Saint Matthew's Passion.* Others include Richter and Rostropovich, Ravel and Stravinsky, Von Karajan and Boulez.

Three different examples of spectacular modernista architecture: left, the unmistakeable façade of the Hospital de Sant Pau; above, the glittering interior of the Palau de la Música Catalana; below, the crenellated castle that houses the Zoological Museum.

Zoological Museum

The museum's beginnings date back to 1882 when Francesco Martorell i Peña donated his personal collections of natural history and archaeology to the city of Barcelona together with a large sum of money to pay for a suitable building to house them. The museum is now located in the eccentric *Castell dels Tres Dragons* (Castle of the Three Dragons) designed by Lluís Domènech i Montaner as a restaurant and bar for the Universal Exhibition in 1888. On the first floor of the museum are the permanent collections such as 'The World of Bees', 'Urban Birdlife' and the 'Classification of the Animal World'. The museum also has a library of zoological sound recordings consisting of over 2,200 registrations of 550 different species covering birds, mammals, amphibians, reptiles and invertebrates typical of European fauna.

Casa Amatller

"The apotheosis of the decorative arts" is how the critic Alexandre Cirici Pellicer described the façade of this building, standing beside *Casa Batlló* and redesigned by Puig i Cadafalch for the chocolate manufacturer Antonio Amatller between 1898 and 1900. As is so typical of his style, the architect has mixed and combined architectural and decorative styles drawn from both Catalan culture and other European countries. Indeed easily recognisable is the Flemish style of the triangular façades that flank the canals in Amsterdam, as well as the gothic style of the window arches and the heavy baroque of the wrought iron decorations.

Casa Macaya

The businessman Roman Macaya i Gibert commissioned Puig i Cadafalch to build this house, designed around a large central courtyard, in 1901. Located on the edge of the *Eixample*, on the *Avinguda Diagonal*, a curious decorative item here represents an interesting story; while he was working on this house Cadafalch was also working on *Casa Amatller* as well as a third house on the *Ramblas* and he travelled between all three on his bicycle. As a joke, therefore, the sculptor Arnau engraved a bicycle on one of the capitals to the left of the main entrance.

Casa Martí (Els 4 Gats - The 4 Cats)

The 'Chat Noir' in Paris and 'Els 4 Gats' in Barcelona were two important points of reference for avant-garde painters and intellectuals in France and Spain respectively. Originally built as the *Casa Martí* by Cadafalch, on 12 June 1897 Pere Romeu and the well-known painter Ramón Casas turned it into a café called 'The 4 Cats' - a name it earned from the Catalan painter Santiago Rusiñol who claimed that only 4 cats would bother to frequent it. Instead, the café was a success: concerts, exhibitions and theatre performances were held here and it became the headquarters of the literary and artistic movement known as the *Renaixença*. In 1899 Picasso was an avid frequenter of the bar with the poet Sabartés, the painter Junyer-Vidal and Carlos Casagemas, who went to Paris with him. This was a period of immense and original artistic fervour and it is perhaps no surprise that the menu and the *affiches* was designed by the great Pablo Picasso.

Pablo Picasso was a keen frequentor of 'Els 4 Gats' and he designed the *affiches* and the first menu of this intriguing new bar. With his unique and sublime touch even in this simple everyday item he managed to transmit the enthusiasm felt for art nouveau – the dominant artistic movement in Barcelona at the time.

Previous page: above, Casa Amatller with its unusual façade and, below, the elaborate façade of Casa Macaya.

Below, interior of the unusually-named bar, 'The 4 Cats' ('El 4 Gats').

The unmistakable torrets of the Casa de les Punxes.

Casa de les Punxes

Built between 1903 and 1905 and also on the *Avingu-da Diagonal* this is one of the most enchanting build-ings of 20th century Barcelona. In designing this build-ing with its vaguely medieval air, Puig i Cadafalch was inspired by a northern architectural style, reminiscent also of some of the castles in the Loire Valley. The exterior is in red brick, however, one of the most familiar hallmarks of modernism and is enhanced by the elegant and elaborate stone decorations of the doors and windows. The building is named after the impressive spires that, shaped like a witches hat, soar up from the corner towers while the upper part of the structure is elegantly decorated with mosaics and ceramics.

Palau del Baró de Quadras

Extending between two important streets of the city – the imposing *Avinguda Diagonal* and *Carrer Rosselló* – this impressive building was commissioned from Puig I Cadafalch in 1900 by Baron de Quadras as his new private residence in Barcelona. Completed between 1904 and 1906, it has two quite different façades: the main façade on *Avinguda Diagonal* is highly decorative and is clearly Gothic in style; the other is much more sombre and, in general, more conventional. The interior was inspired by the splendours of Islamic art and in fact provides the perfect setting for the **Museum of Music** that opened here in 1983 exhibiting historical musical instruments from all over the world.

The Gothic façade of Palau del Baró de Quadras.

MUSEU DE LA MÚSICA

The Barcelona *Museum of Music* is almost 60 years old and can boast a collection that is quite unique in Spain consisting not only of musical instruments but also documents, scores and signed letters and manuscripts. The main purposes of the museum are to promote the conservation and diffusion of the vast heritage of Spanish music and to provide a unique point of reference for the research and teaching of music with materials, documents and other services. Housed in the *Palau del Baró de Quadras*, a masterpiece of *modernista* architecture, the museum has an important *collection of European musical instruments* dating from the 16th to the 20th century, as well as a suberb collection of *guitars* documenting the most traditional Spanish musical instrument and including a wealth of documentation relating specifically to Catalan musicians and composers. Other sections are dedicated to various aspects of different musical cultures found around the world. The construction of the new Barcelona Auditorium may provide a new more suitable - and hopefully definitive - home for this interesting museum.

The musical instruments are one of the most prestigious collections belonging to the Museu de la Música, located in the Palau del Baró de Quadras.

ART IN THE STREETS

CONTINUALLY SURPRIS-
ING, INNOVATIVE AND AT-
TENTIVE TO THE MOST RAD-
ICAL NOTIONS, BARCELONA
HAS SUCEEDED IN CREATING A
GENUINE OPEN AIR MUSEUM
IN THE STREETS, SQUARES AND
PARKS. THE WORKS ARE BY SOME
OF THE GREATEST MODERN
ARTISTS FROM EUROPE AND BE-
YOND, AND IN PARTICULAR JOAN
MIRÓ, TO WHOM THE ENTIRE
AREA OF THE OLD CITY SLAUGH-
TERHOUSE IS DEDICATED. LARGE
AND IMPORTANT SCULPTURES
ARE DISPLAYED IN KEY LOCA-
TIONS AND THESE TRUELY ORIG-
INAL WORKS OF ART LEND AN
UNUSUAL AND HIGHLY COLOUR-
FUL TOUCH TO THE EXISTING
URBAN ENVIRONMENT.

Joan Miró, the "greatest surrealist of us all" as André Breton, the father of surrealism, defined him, is the author of the sculpture Dona i Ocell, a symbolically phallic totem in concrete and coloured ceramic mosaic.

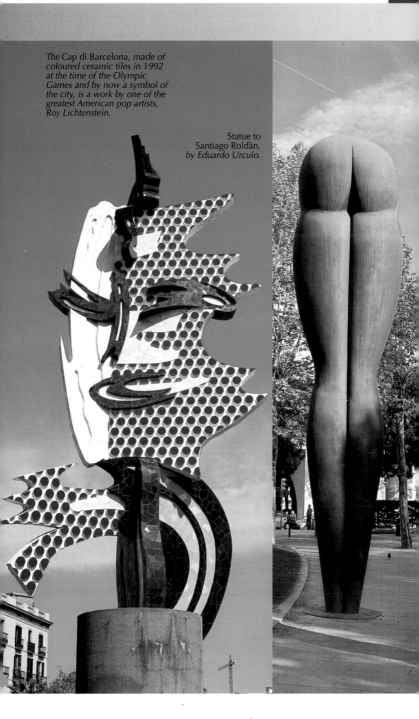

The Cap di Barcelona, *made of coloured ceramic tiles in 1992 at the time of the Olympic Games and by now a symbol of the city, is a work by one of the greatest American pop artists,* Roy Lichtenstein.

Statue to Santiago Roldàn, *by Eduardo Urculo.*

ART IN THE STREETS

Above left, Mistos – gigantic matches by the Swede Claes Oldenburg and his wife, Coosje van Bruggen in steel, aluminium, reinforced plastic and enamelled polyeurethane. Above right, the immense Peixe (Fish) 54 metres long and 35 high at the entrance to the Olympic Port, by the Canadian Frank Gehry who designed the Guggenheim Museum in Bilbao. At the beginning of the 1980s, Gehry's sculptures were much inspired by nature: referring to fish he stated that he "was fascinated by the perfection and variety of their many forms". Left, original dynamic sculpture by the Basque artist Andrés Nagel called Drac with a slide for children concealed inside. The sculpture is located in the Spanish Industrial Park, a name that recalls the textile industry that once flourished there.

ART IN THE STREETS

On the right, David and Goliath / Goliath and David by Antoni Llena, 25 metres high made of tubular steel and sheet metal, in the Parc de les Cascades. Below, Monument to the Book, by Joan Brossa, standing at a busy corner of the Gran Via.

Above, Autovia by Josep Maria Subirachs, one of the most famous living Catalan artists, currently working on the atrium of the Passion Façade of the Sagrada Familia. Below, El Gato by Fernando Botero, the famous Colombian sculptor and painter born in Medellín in 1932.

CATALUNYA A LA CIUTAT DE BARCELONA. DESEMBRE DE MCMXCIV

Brossa

MONTJUÏC

The hill of Montjuïc is one of the most interesting areas of the city and has always been a strategic point of defence. In 1640, after the "dels Segadors" war against Philip IV, the city of Barcelona built a military fortification, the **Citadel** or **Castle**, on the top of Montjuïc. When the city surrendered to Philip V's Bourbon armies at the end of the unfortunate War of Succession to the Spanish throne, the Castle was transformed into a military prison. Only recently in the early 1960s did the army hand the old Castle over to the city. The Castle now houses a *Museum of Military History* with antique weapons, mementos of the battle of Lepanto, relics of Catalan and Arab history and whole armies of lead soldiers. A marvelous panorama of Barcelona can be had from the bastions of the Castle. The hill of Montjuïc which surrounds the Citadel has quite magnificent: gardens, monuments, an amusement park, museums and palaces making it an irresistible attraction for tourists and locals. Montjuïc

owes its present splendour to the ability of the architect Amargós and the French landscape architect Forestier, and the work done to prepare for the 1929 International Exhibition. Along the avenues of Montjuïc are the **Palau Nacional**, built

The splendid view of Barcelona from the hill of Montjuïc and below left, the fortified entrance to the old Castle.

expressly for the Exhibition, the ***Pabellón de la Rosaleda*** which houses the **Ethnological Museum**, the **Archaeological Museum**, a Greek theatre, the botanical gardens, the *Font del Gat*, the reconstructions of the *Poble Espanyol*, the **Fundació Joan Miró**, Centre of Research for the Contemporary Arts, and the ***Miramar***, which dominates the entire city.

THE SARDANA

"La sardana es la danza más bella de todas las danzas que se hacen y deshacen, es el móvil, magnífico anillo que con pausa y con medida va lento oscilando".
(Joan Maragall, *Elogi de la Sardana*)

The choral dance of the *Sardana* exhibits the essence of the Catalan people and of Barcelona itself. On the hill of Montjuïc is the monument by sculptor José Cañas to the *Sardana* — a dance that every Catalonian knows how to perform perfectly.

THE JOAN MIRÓ FOUNDATION

On June 10,1975, Joan Miró made Barcelona the best of all possible gifts: the Foundation which bears his name, the *Fundació Joan Miró, Centre d'Estudis d'Art Contemporani,* opened providing a cultural centre that has raised Catalonia to the highest levels of world art.

The building which houses the Foundation is on the hill of Montjuïc and was designed by Joan Prats and the architect Josep-Lluís Sert and in 1976 a large exhibition of 475 drawings (covering the period 1901 to 1975) marked its formal inauguration.

In 1978 the Council of Europe awarded the Miró Foundation the "Special Prize for a Museum", an international acknowledgment of the imaginative work of the Catalan painter. Miró himself stated that "What is closest to my heart is Catalonia and the dignity of man".

The Foundation's collection has some 11,000 items mostly donated by the artist: 240 paintings, 175 sculptures, 9 tapestries, 4 ceramic works, almost all the graphic works and about 8,000 drawings. The core collection is arranged in different rooms: the *Sculpture Room*, the *Tapestry Room*, the *Joan Prats Room*, the *1960s and 70s Room*, as well as

JOAN MIRÓ

It has been said that "Joan Miró is the night, silence, music". And Joan Miró, one of the greatest artists of our century, appreciated the definition recognizing himself in it. He was born in Barcelona on 20th April 1893 in *Passatge del Crédit*, number 4. The capital of Catalonia and the entire region strongly influenced him. Chagall, the Russian painter in exile in Paris, one day wrote to him: "You are lucky, my boy, you have a country". But Joan Miró never tolerated the fact that art books or encyclopedias defined him as a "Spanish painter". He sent endless letters of protest, demanding - and succeeding - in being called a "Catalan painter".

Joan Miró began to paint at an early age. A friend of Picabia, Max Ernst and André Masson, an impassioned habitué of the Dadaists, he knew Hemingway, Ezra Pound, Jacques Prévert, Henry Miller, and, above all, Breton, Éluard and Aragon.

He exhibited for the first time in Barcelona in 1918. A year later he moved to Paris where he adhered to the cubist movement though in 1924 he passed into the ranks of the surrealists. But perhaps it is not really possible to catalogue Miró's art: Miró is unmistakeable, his hand moves in absolute freedom. Giulio Carlo Argan, the Italian art historian, defined him as "the nightingale of modern painting". The artist always moved beyond the frontiers of the rational and the senses to create one of the richest and most fascinating styles of artistic expressions of the 20th-century.

Joan Miró died in Palma di Maiorca on Christmas Day 1983 aged 90. He is buried in Barcelona.

the large roof terrace which provides a stupendous setting.

But this continually dynamic Foundation also maintains other activities: temporary exhibitions of modern artists are held, musical and children's events are organised and debates and discussions take place to "re-think art today".

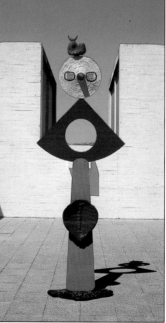

Some of Miró's most important works, the pride of the Foundation named after him in Barcelona, and housed in a gleaming white structure built specifically for the purpose, illustrated below left. Note in particular the bronze sculptures such as, below right, the Caress of a Bird, dated 1967. This was the year in which Miró began to add colour to the works in bronze producing brightly coloured statues. Personage (above left) and Monument (left) both date from 1970.

121

MUSEU NACIONAL D'ART DE CATALUNYA (MNAC)

Situated on the hill of Montjuïc, overlooking the *Plaça de Espanya* below, the Palace of the 1929 International Exhibition houses on its ground floor the Art Museum of Catalonia, with probably the richest collection in the world of Romanesque Catalan art and certainly one of the most important of Gothic panel paintings and sculptures. Created by Josep Lluís Pellicer, it was enlarged by his successor Joaquí Folch y Torres, who also enriched it with numerous frescoes from various churches and convents in northern Catalonia. The more important works preserved in the rooms dedicated to Romanesque art include the frescoes from the Church of Sant Joan de Bohí (*Martyrdom of St. Stephen*), the detached frescoes from the apse of the Church of San Clemente de Tahull, representing *Christ Pantokrator,* the *Virgin* and the *Apostles* (12th cent.), and those from the churches of Santa María de Tahull, Santa María de Aneu and San Ginestarre de Cardós (12th cent.). A group of works attributed to the so-called Master of Pedret, datable to the 11th-12th century and characterized by motifs close to Byzantine art, are also of particular interest. Noteworthy among the many wooden altar frontals in the museum are one from Seu d'Urgell, Santa María de Tahull in polychrome relief (both 12th cent.) representing *God the Father in Majesty*, one from Valltarga, and one from Sorriguerola, which already marks the passage from the Romanesque to the Gothic. This later period is well represented by a fine series of retablos, including one from Santa Coloma de Queralt attributed to Juan de Tarragona, and the *retablo de Sigena,* by the Serra brothers. The most significant moments in Catalan art are represented by Lluís Borrassá (*Resurrection,* first half of the 15th cent.), with whom Catalan art became receptive to various international influences; Lluís Dalmau, who was influenced by Flemish art (*Altarpiece of the Councillors,* 1445), and the famous Jaume Huguet (1436-1486), skillful interpreter of Flemish naturalism in Catalan art at the end of the 15th century (*Consecration of St. Augustine*).

The majestic Palace of the International Exhibition (actually Palau Nacional) on the hill of Montjuïc, home to the Catalonia Art Museum.

Spanish painting of the 16th and 17th centuries is also well represented, with works by Pedro Berruguete, Velázquez, El Greco and Zurbarán. Also housed here is the **Cambò Collection** donated by the banker and statesman Francesc Cambò, and containing various works by famous artists, ranging from pre-renaissance painting up to more recent times. The collections of the **Ceramic Museum** are also exhibited in this complex.

Some examples of frescoes preserved in the museum, including (right) Christ Pantokrator (12th century) and, below, a mural decoration for a burial (11th century).

MUSEU D'ARQUEOLOGIA DE CATALUNYA

The collections of the Archaeological Museum are exhibited in what was originally the *Palace of Graphic Arts* built for the International Exhibition of 1929 and also situated in the park of Montjuïc. The Museum is dedicated to the ancient civilizations of the Mediterranean, and its collections fill more than 30 rooms where items are exhibited chronologically, ranging in time from prehistory to the 8th century. *Rooms I-X* contain prehistoric material dating from the stone age. Worthy of note are the examples of pottery from Guadix and the reconstructions of the most important dolmens to be found in Spain. *Rooms XI-XIII* contain Bronze Age jewellery found in the Balearic Islands. *Room XIV* contains Greek, Punic and pre-Roman pottery. Of particular note is *Room XV,* containing a survey of the items that came to light during the excavations in Ampuries. Outstanding are the Greek statues of *Venus* and *Aesculapius,* as well as the Roman mosaic of *Iphigeneia. Rooms XVI-XVII* contain collections of pottery from the Mediterranean basin, in particular the Greek, Italiote and Etruscan areas. There are also examples of Roman and Hellenistic sculpture, as well as fragments of Etruscan and Roman fresco paintings. *Room XVIII* contains pottery of varied provenance, particularly Greek, Apulian and Campanian, ranging from the 6th to the 4th centuries B.C. *Room XIX* houses interesting examples of Etruscan bucchero from the 7th and 6th centuries B.C. *Rooms XX-XXIII* are dedicated to artefacts from the Iberian and Roman areas (applied arts). Exhibited in *Rooms XXIV-XXVI* are interesting examples of Roman mosaic art. Of particular note are the representations of the *Race in the Circus* and the *Three Graces. Rooms XXVII-XXXI* house the reconstruction of

The majestic statue of Aesculapius in the Archaeological Museum.

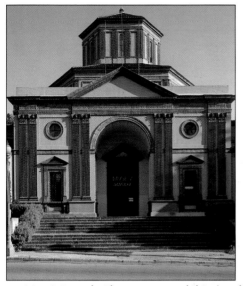

a Roman house. Various sarcophagi of early Christian date are to be found in *Room XXXIII* while fine examples of Visigothic goldsmithing are on view in the vestibule.

MUSEU ETNOLÒGIC

The collections of the Ethnological Museum are housed in a modern building surrounded by the gardens of the Montjuïc park. The museum exhibits artefacts, objects of daily use, crafts and costumes from Oceania, various regions of Asia, Africa and the Americas, collected over centuries in the course of numerous Spanish expeditions. Of particular importance are the materials from pre- and post-Columbian cultures, though there are also examples from the Australian aboriginal culture. Also worth a visit are the Japanese ceramics and objects from Senegal and Morocco.

The main entrance to the Archaeological Museum housed in what was the graphic arts palace at the time of the International Exhibition; below, the modern building where the Ethnological Museum is located.

125

PAVELLÒ MIES VAN DER ROHE

Designed by Mies van der Rohe (1886-1969) as the German Pavilion for the 1929 International Exhibition, and dismantled six months after, the building nevertheless became a point of reference and source of inspiration for generations of archictects everywhere. Made with marble, travertine and glass, the building was remarkable for its classic rationality. Such was the interest and enthusiasm that the structure continued to evoke it was decided as part of the celebrations of the centenary of the designer's birth, to rebuild it exactly as and where it had originally been, also reviving the entire context for which it had been built. Work began in 1983 and was completed three

years later. Today the pavilion still represents a complete synthesis of the architectural style of this great director of the Bauhaus; the walls in reddish marble and onyx are lightened by the flat roof covering, while the two pools of water reflect the play of light and shadow created by the pillars of chromium-plated steel and the smooth stone. The pavilion is open to the public and houses the **Fundació Mies van der Rohe**. Inaugurated in 1983, the Foundation houses an excellent library related to the works of Mies van der Rohe, organises conferences and exhibitions and promotes research and documentation of the cultural aspects of modern architecture.

The superb linearity of the architecture is one of the main elements of the modern beauty of the Mies van der Rohe Pavilion.

GEORG KOLBE (1877-1947)

Born in Waldheim in Saxony, Georg Kolbe was one of the most important German sculptors of the early 20th century and strongly influenced other artists of his generation, especially as regards the idealistic interpretation of the nude. After studying painting and drawing in Dresden, Munich and Paris (1891-1898), he was in Rome between 1898 and 1901. On returning to Germany he had acquired a complete awareness of the theoretical studies which would help him to develop his own expressive style with greater skill and individuality over the next decade. A member of the Prussian Academy of Arts and by then well established both as a painter and sculptor, Kolbe was continually capable of stimulating great interest in his work, profoundly influenced over time by historical events (First World War, Weimar Republic, Third Reich, Second World War) and those in his personal life (the tragic death of his wife in 1927). Entirely in harmony with the geometric architecture of Mies van der Rohe, one of his sculptures — *Morning*, dated 1925 — is displayed in what was the German Pavilion of the 1929 Barcelona International Exhibition, its smoothly classic linearity contributing perfectly to the atmosphere of relaxing and reflective calm.

Morning by Georg Kolbe.

The Magic Fountain is also the fountain of fantastic numbers: the main body consists of two concentric basins at different heights; the water arrives at the fountain at the rate of 2,430 litres a second; the jet of water reaches, and at times exceeds, fifty metres in height. Pumps and fans using 1,413 steam horsepower and 4,730 bulbs employing 1,445 kilowatts are an indication of the energy needed to set it in motion. In this particular version of "Son et Lumière" Barcelona has outdone itself. Using remote control, an operator in a cabin directs the play of lights in the Magic Fountain all summer long.

PALAU NACIONAL

Two unusual towers of pure Venetian style form the entrance to the area where the International Exhibition was located in 1929. The two towers lead to the spacious *Avinguda de la Reina María Cristina*, a wide avenue designed by the architect Raventós. The perspective of the boulevard is daring: the various Exhibition buildings lead in a rapid series from *Plaça de Espanya* up to the extraordinary ornamental waterworks of the fountain by Carles Buigas. In the background, on the slopes of the hill of Montjuïc, rises the austere mass of the *Palau Nacional*, facing the mount on which the Sanctuary of Tibidabo rises.

The fountain, situated at the foot of the flight of stairs that leads to the Palau Nacional, was made by the engineer, Carles Buigas. Known simply as the "Luminous Fountain", it is also called the *Magic Fountain* of Barcelona. And rightly so: on hot summer nights its ornamental waterworks and lights illuminate the entire city with the kaleidoscope of its reflections. The number of variations and imaginative combinations come close to thirty composing a chromatic mosaic, an unending rainbow. At the top of the steps leading up from the enchantment of the fountain lies the *Palau Nacional,* whose rooms contain the collections of the *Museu Nacional d'Art de Catalunya.* The *Palau Nacional* was also designed by Buigas for the 1929 International Exhibition and it housed at the time the section dedicated to electricity.

Palau Nacional with the stupendous display created by the Magic Fountain.

The two soaring towers, inspired by the belltower of Saint Mark's in Venice, stand between Palau Nacional and the Plaça de Espanya. Below, the monumental fountain that stands at the centre of the square.

PLAÇA DE ESPANYA - One of the most convulsive and noisy intersections in Barcelona, *Plaça de Espanya* is situated at the crossing of *Avinguda Gran Via de les Corts Catalanes* and *Avinguda del Paral-lel (Calle del Marqués del Duero)*. Now overflowing with traffic this immense and impressive square was originally the monumental entrance to the area of the International Exhibition of 1929. The monumental *fountain* at the centre of the square is by Catalan architect Jujol, one of Gaudí's best pupils. The three statues by Oslé which decorate the triangular structure symbolically represent the waters of the three seas which bathe the coasts of Spain – the *Mediterranean,* the *Bay of Biscay* (or *Mar Cantabricum)* and the *Atlantic Ocean.* The principal airlines have their headquarters in *Plaça de Espanya* and the Air Iberia terminal is located there. Here too is the second *Plaça de Toros* in Barcelona, *Les Arenes:* built in the latter part of the 19th century it can seat up to 26,000 spectators. The three massive red brick buildings in the square were hotels built to accommodate the visitors to the 1929 Exhibition.

POBLE ESPANYOL - The *Poble Espanyol* is an entertaining 'Spain-in-miniature' extending over two hectares on the hill of Montjuïc. The streets, squares, houses and buildings faithfully reproduce various important and characteristic Gothic and renaissance parts of cities and localities in Catalonia, Aragon, Andalusia, Galicia, Castile, the Balearic Islands, Navarre and Estremadura. It was created for the 1929 International Exhibition by Xavier Nogués, Miquel Utrillo and Ramón Raventós.

The replicas, constructed and arranged with amazing attention to detail, provide a complete anthology of Spanish architecture and of the extremely diverse architectural features of the regions of the north, the south, the mountains and the coast. Two impressive towers of the *Puerta de San Vicente* (or *Puerta de Ávila*) stand at the entrance to the village. The walls which enclose the village and which reproduce the walls of the city of Avila begin here. Entering by the gate we find *"Plaza Castellana"*, to the right of which, in *"Calle de la Conquista"*, are buildings representing those of Cáceres. Passing under the portico of Sangüesa, we come to the *Plaza Mayor,* surrounded by buildings that are typical of Guadalajara, Madrid, Segovia, Santander, etc. The square also contains a reproduction of the city

Every street in the most original 'Poble Espanyol' is a fascinating and intriguing voyage of discovery, from Puerta San Vicente (left) to the Santiago Stairway (below left) and the vast and unusual Plaza Mayor (above).

hall of Vall-de-roures. To the left of the *Plaza Mayor*, after *"Calle del Alcalde de Zalamea"* is the *Santiago Stairway* and other impressive Galician buildings while further on in *Plaza Aragonesa*, the bell tower of the church of Utebo in a picturesque moorish style rises to the sky. The charming reconstruction of the simple Andalusian style begins here, followed by the Catalan quarter where an old pharmacy is also reproduced. Retracing one's steps to *Plaza Mayor* and turning into *"Calle de los Caballeros"*, the road leads to the area dedicated to the simple and austere rural buildings of Castile, beyond which we find dwellings that recall the Basque and Navarre regions.

Plaza Mayor frequently provides a marvellous setting for exhibitions and folklore festivals. *Casa Pallaresa* on the square houses one of the most important museums in the village, the *Museu d'Arts, Indústries i Tradicions Populars*, dedicated to the customs and traditions of Catalonia. Nearby, the *Museum of Graphic Arts* provides an interesting survey of printing methods and graphic techniques.

The village abounds in small shops specialized in the sale of typical regional products and where the visitor can watch as craft objects in clay, glass, wrought iron and wood are made.

A visit to the Romanesque *Monastery* beyond the city walls is well worthwhile. Its frescoes reproduce typical pictorial decorations of the small Catalan churches in the Pyrenees.

BARCELONA OLYMPIC CITY

With the proclamation of Barcelona as the site of the 1992 Olympic Games, the city witnessed the completion of many great reforms and improvements. The communications network reflects these important changes and innovations: new road tunnels, broad city streets, promenades such as the *Paseo Picasso,* boulevards such as the *Avenida Gaudí,* but also motorways and ring roads. The city is now able to enjoy new parks such as *Collserola* and *Vall d'Hebron.* The railway network has been modified and the airport enlarged.

One of the most surprising results is undoubtedly the construction of the new district known as *Nova Icària,* which takes its name from Etienne Cabet's Utopian idea of founding an ideal city. Set between the Park of the Citadel (*Parc de la Ciutadella*) and the Cemetery of Poblenou (*Cementiri del Poblenou*), this new *Parc de Mar* district is part of one of the four Olympic areas. During the Games, the area hosted the Olympic Village where the participating athletes and their entourages were housed. But undoubtedly, the nerve centre for the '92 Barcelona Olympic Games was the area of Montjuïc, entirely reorganised in order to house a major part of the sports facilities. The **Olympic Ring** is the name given to the reurbanization of an extensive rocky area that was integrated into the city. The old stadium that dated back to the 1929 International Exhibition was rebuilt, though its façade was preserved, and is now Olympic size with its capacity extended to seat about 60,000 people. The *Sant Jordi Palace* (*Palau Sant Jordi*), a pavilion designed by the architect Arata Isozaki for gymnastics, can seat 17,000 spectators and is a marvel, both from an architectural and a technological point of view. New constructions included the *Industrial Spain Pavilion* (*Pavellò de la*

Above, Palau Sant Jordi, an elegant sports structure by the architect Isozaki and below, the modern Olympic Stadium.

SANTIAGO CALATRAVA

Santiago Calatrava was born in 1951 in Valencia and studied at the School of Art and the Faculty of Architecture there. After his degree, in 1975 he went to Zurich to study civil engineering at the Polytechnic. On qualifying in 1979 he started work as an assistant, first at the Institute of Statics and then at the Institute of Light Structures. He opened a studio in Zurich in 1981, began to participate in competitions and won his first commissions for Spain and Switzerland, including the highly important design of the Stadelhofen station in Zurich. Its completion in 1990 won him recognition on the international scene and enabled him to open a second studio in Paris. Also during this period Calatrava was given the opportunity to design a challenging structure in the heart of the Olympic city that was coming into being.

The communications tower (1989-1991) he was commissioned to design is a futuristic masterpiece in gleaming steel, now named the *Calatrava Tower* (right) brightly soaring high on the hill of Montjuïc.

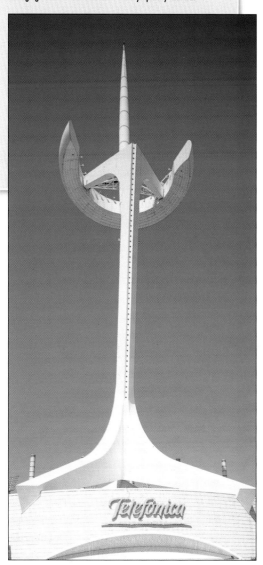

Espanya Industrial), situated within an urban park, the *Metallurgy Palace* (*Palau de la Metallùrgica*), that at present is part of the exhibition complex, and the *Pavilion of the Institute of Physical Education of Catalonia* (*Pavellò de l'Institut Nacional d'Educaciò Fisica de Catalunya*). Completing the Montjuïc district are buildings belonging to the exhibition complex and the *Municipal Sports Hall* (*Palau Municipal d'Esports*).

S U R R O U

THE STADIUM AND FOOTBALL TEAM

THE AMAZING URBAN DEVELOPMENT THAT BARCELONA HAS UNDERGONE SINCE THE 1980S HAS SEEN THE CITY EXPAND RAPIDLY TOWARDS THE WEST AND TOWARDS THE SURROUNDING HILLS, BRINGING ABOUT A THE REDISCOVERY AND REDIMENSIONING OF MANY AREAS. THUS IN THE UPPER PART OF THE CITY, RESIDENTIAL AREAS HAVE DEVELOPED AROUND THE *AREA DE LA DIAGONAL* WHERE *CAMP NOU* AND THE *SARRIÀ STADIUM* REPRESENT TWO OF THE MOST MODERN SPORTS COMPLEXES. AND EVEN HIGHER UP, THE *PEDRABLES MONASTRY* AND *PALAU REIAL* ARE TWO HISTORICAL TREASURES WHILE *TIBIDABO* IS A FAVOURITE AREA FOR A TRIP OUT OF THE CITY.

And a splendid team required a splendid stadium. *Camp Nou* is the largest in Europe with capacity for 100,000 spectators and is the pride of the entire city both for its architectural design and the modernity of the sporting facilities.

When, on 29 November 1899 Hans Gamper, a Swiss, placed an advert in a local paper to recruit football players he could hardly have imagined that from the 11 selected, one of the most famous and acclaimed teams in the world would come into being. As the motto states, *"Més que un club"*, it would be more than a football club, becoming a real icon, a religion, a symbol of political and cultural identity. *"Visca el Barça"* is not only a slogan chanted from the terraces of *Camp Nou* by the supporters to spur on their team, it is also a passionate rivendication of the rivalry (not just in football!) with the eternal enemy, Real Madrid.

NOT ONLY FOOTBALL – *Camp Nou* is not only used for sporting events but it is also frequently the scene of important occasions that attract tens of thousands of spectators. As well as concerts with Bruce Springsteen and Michael Jackson, Julio Iglesias and the three tenors – Carreras, Domingo and Pavarotti – the stadium has also hosted the high mass held before 120,000 faithful by Pope John Paul II on 7 November 1982. On this occasion the Pope was awarded membership card number 108,000 by the club's president!

*Above right,
the fabulous Camp Nou in Barcelona.*

N D I N G S

BARCELONA F. C. MUSEUM – PRESIDENT NUÑEZ

The idea of dedicating a museum to Barcelona Football Club, dates back to 1920 and to Joan Gamper. The dream only became reality in 1984 however, thanks to the then President, Nuñez. The museum is organised in several sections, including history (trophies, photos, audiovisuals), art (works by Dalí, Miró, Subirachs) and documents (a library, newspapers and periodicals collection and photo archive).

The strength of Barcelona Football Club can also be seen in its impressive record: 24 King's Cup, 16 League Cups, 2 European Cups, 5 Spanish League Cups, 3 UEFA Cups, 4 Cup Winners Cups and the fabulous Champion's Cup on 21 May 1992.

PALAU REIAL DE PEDRALBES

Pedralbes is one of the wealthiest residential districts in the city, where art nouveau buildings stand side by side with elegant villas and dignified constructions of more recent date. In any case the green of the hedges and gardens is the predominating note.

The *Palau Reial de Pedralbes* is in the University City, near the end of *Avinguda Diagonal* and was built between 1919 and 1929 as a residence for Alfonso XIII, king of Spain, in a style inspired by Italian renaissance palaces. Currently used as a residence for heads of State or other important visitors, it is open to the public and surrounded by an enchanting park. Beside the *Museu de Cerámica*, is the **Museu d'Arts Decoratives**, opened in 1932, created from various private collections and later increased by a series of important donations. The various sections cover: period furnishings, embroidery, textiles, Flanders tapestries, objects in glass from the pre-Roman period to the 18th century, porcelain, an interesting collection of carriages, and a recent collection (1995) based on Spanish design and industrial engineering. A guided visit allows us to admire the rich decoration of the interiors (outstanding is the sumptuous *Throne Room,* with

Palau Reial de Pedralbes: above, the entrance to the palace from the gardens, below, the sumptuous Throne Room and one of the bedrooms.

its vault entirely decorated with imitation architecture), the furnishings, in part from Italy, and the valuable collections of porcelain, clocks, tapestries, fans and paintings (some by Luca Giordano).

REIAL MONESTIR DE PEDRALBES

This monastery, one of the most evocative of ancient Barcelona, was founded by Queen Elisenda de Montcada, fourth and last wife of Jaime II. It was built between 1326 and

The exterior of Reial Monestir de Pedralbes, with the sturdy octagonal tower and a corner of the cloister, showing the elegant garden.

1419 by Ferrer Peiró and by Domènec Granyer and is one of the finest remaining examples of Catalan Gothic. Not all of the monastery is open to the public as the Order of Saint Claire occupies part of it. Noteworthy, on the exterior of the church, is the fine octagonal tower and, on the façade, the emblems of the Montcada family. Inside, the single majestic nave with 14th-century stained-glass windows contains the monumental *tomb of Queen Elisenda* with an alabaster figure representing the queen. The *Chapter House* is also fine, ornamented with a stained-glass window from the first half of the 15th century. The airy cloister, with three orders of galleries supported by elegant small columns, leads to the *Chapel of Sant Miquel,* with its splendid frescoes of the *Stories of the Life of the Virgin,* by Ferrer Bassa (1290-1348), one of the greatest Catalan painters and illuminators of the 14th century. Also active for some years in Italy, Bassa has endowed the ecstatic figures in the various scenes, dominated by a uniform blue ground, with various elements derived from contemporary Sienese and Giottesque painting. Dating to 1343, the paintings are well preserved. The convent also houses a *museum* dedicated to medieval painting and sculpture and to liturgical objects, as well as an important part of the Von Thyssen collection – one of the largest and most complete in the world – which has been acquired by the Spanish state.

TIBIDABO

Tibidabo is the highest summit (over 500 metres) of *Collserola*, the hills surrounding the city and protecting it from the winds of the north.

An overall panorama can be had from this modest crest, which can be reached by bus, cable car or by car. It includes the entire city with the ocean in the background, the other summits of the chain (such as "*La Arrabassada*" and "*Sant Pere Mártir*"), as well as Montserrat, and beyond, the summits of the Pyrenees.

Halfway down its green slopes are the **Astronomical Observatory** and the **Museum of Physical Sciences**, which were created early in the 20th century thanks to Camilo Fabra, marquis of Alella. The crest of Tibidabo is crowned by the majestic **Church of the Sacred Heart**, built in Gothic style by the architect Enric Sagnier. An elevator inside the church further extends the already vast panorama offered by Tibidabo. On the highest spire of the building a *Statue of Jesus* with widespread arms seems to lean out

The stupendous panoramic view from Tibidabo sweeping across the city to the boundless horizon of the sea. Following page, above, the Astronomical Observatory, clinging to the slopes of Tibidabo and the futuristic Collserola Tower.

NORMAN FOSTER

Born in Manchester in 1935, Norman Foster is considered one of the foremost representatives of 'high tech' architecture. After taking a degree at Manchester University, he completed his Masters Degree at Yale University where he met Richard Rogers, another English student destined to become an important figure in contemporary architecture. On their return to England (1963) Foster and Rogers established a studio called 'Team 4' with Su Rogers and Wendy Foster. In 1967 Norman and Wendy Foster created 'Foster Associates', today known as 'Foster and Partners' with about 500 employees. Among the studio's most recent projects are the Millennium Bridge in London and the new international airport in Hong Kong.

over the underlying city. Tibidabo is a favorite outing, with an *Amusement Park* as one of its attractions. Surrounded by terraces, avenues, large squares, and charming gardens, the roller coaster, the labyrinth, the haunted house, numerous bars and attractive restaurants create an ideal atmosphere for relaxation and entertainment.

Of the many attractions Tibidabo offers, particular mention must be made of the unique **Museum of Automaton** which contains a large number of robots, automatized machines and automa from every corner of the globe, dating to a wide variety of periods. In the immediate vicinity of Tibidado, one of the many interesting houses that merit mention is the *Villa Joana*, now the **Casa-Museu Verdaguer**, created in homage to the contemporary Catalan poet M. J. Verdaguer, who lived there until his death. The villa is surrounded by the large green *Park of Vallvidrera*. Also of interest is the **Collserola Tower** (Barcelona's telecommunications tower) inaugurated at the time of the Olympic Games and designed by Norman Foster. It is 288 metres high with 13 'platforms'. The **Mirador** is located on the 10th level and is reached in a panoramic elevator that rises 135 metres in less than two minutes. The view from the *Mirador* sweeps over the entire city and may reach up to 70 kilometres in clear weather.

The Church of the Sacred Heart, at the top of Tibidabo, appears dominated by the immense statue of Christ who seems to want to embrace the city.
Following page, the famous funfair with numerous attractions which were entirely renewed in the 1980s.

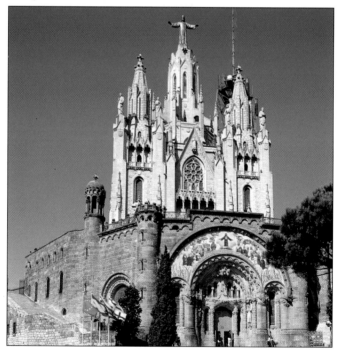

141

The Monastery of Montserrat and on the left, the funicular railway that leads up to the Chapel, designed by Gaudí on the spot where the Madonna appeared. Next page, the monumental staircase (above) and the interior (below right) of the church, where the much venerated "Moreneta" is housed (below left).

MONTSERRAT

The mountain of Montserrat rises about 30 kilometres north of Barcelona. Its highest summit, named after Saint Jerome, is over a thousand metres high. The Catalan term *"Montserrat"*, or *serrated mountain*, is a most suitable name for the appearance of this massive stony ridge, modelled over the centuries by the force of the elements. Montserrat attracts many hikers, as well as numerous enthusiastic tourists. As far back as the 8th century various hermitages existed on Montserrat including the hermitage of S. María, converted by Bishop Oliva in the 11th century into a small monastery, the forerunner of the present sanctuary, which was to become famous throughout Catalonia thanks to the Romanesque statue of a miraculous *Madonna* (12th century), called *"Moreneta"* by the Catalans for the dark colour of her skin. According to legend she appeared in a cave in the mountains. The monastery soon became known all over Europe, and religious buildings dedicated to the Madonna of Montserrat arose everywhere and even one of the Antille islands was given the name of Montserrat. Among the most famous personages connected with the monastery are Giuliano della Rovere (future Pope Julius II), who was responsible for the building of the cloister in Gothic style (1476), the Emperor Ferdinand III, who made generous donations to the Benedictine community, Ignatius of Loyola, Goethe and Schiller, who immortalized the mountain in some of their works.
From the 16th century on, the church, numerous annexes of the

monastery, and buildings for the pilgrims, who increased as the sanctuary became more famous, were added to the original hermitage.

In 1811 the monastery was sacked by the Napoleonic army and the successive revolutionary uprising reduced Montserrat to a pile of ruins abandoned by the monks.

The rapid rebirth of the sanctuary which began in the middle of the 19th century continued despite the Civil War (1936-1939) thanks to the intervention of the autonomous government of Barcelona.

The present monastery rises on a narrow ledge about 700 metres high. The large basilica was built between 1559 and 1592 and is more than 60 metres long and over 30 metres high. The façade, as we see it today, dates to the 1960s. The elegant **interior,** with a single nave scanned by Gothic arches and flanked by side chapels, ends in a richly decorated apse, which dates to the second half of the 19th century. From here a marble staircase leads to the chapel which houses the wooden polychrome statue of the *Madonna of Montserrat* (patron saint of Catalonia since 1881). As well as the large library (containing over 200,000 volumes), the *Museum* has an interesting collection covering the most important periods of European painting, and archaeological items of various origin.

143

CATALA

A TASTE OF THE COUNTRY

In Catalonia you will find aïoli, like that in Provence and Languedoc, spaghetti like that of Naples, and cannelloni like those in Bologna. But you should not think that these dishes are imitations or have been borrowed due to a lack of creativity. On the contrary, these and many other dishes are part of a gastronomical culture in constant evolution, eternally capable of grafting new ideas onto existing forms giving birth to new creations - a culture that can adopt *paella*, born in Valencia, and turn it into *paella parellada* and the delicious *fideua*, using pasta instead of rice. In savouring the tastes and flavours of the region, you will discover that both sophisticated dishes and more rustic, basic meals have their place in the gastronomy of Catalonia, skilled at presenting masterpieces of haute cuisine and originality and old family recipes with the same flair, and at easily combining elements from the two fundamental components of the Catalan landscape - sea and mountains. The food is both sophisticated and familiar, elegant and typical, and you will enjoy with equal pleasure dishes that skillfully combine and harmonise sweet and savoury, making indulgent use of chocolate such as the *estofat de bou*, and the simplest of tastes such as *pan amb tomaquet,* country style bread with garlic and tomato rubbed over it. In the course of time, Catalan cookery has perfected a culinary style that is based on four basics: *picada, romesco, samfaina,* and *sofrito* – these are more than simple sauces to accompany food but, according to historians, the dictates of great international cookery, basic preparations that represent the

foundations of all gastronomic creations. The Catalonian tendancy to synthesize can be seen in the existence of dishes that are difficult to 'classify' according to international conventions (entrée, first course, second course and so on) and seem to belong to all or to none of these categories at the same time. Take, for instance the numerous rice dishes (*arros a banda, arros a la català, arroz con habas* to name but a few) real one-course dishes similar to pasta (*fideos a la catalana, fideos con mariscos* and *fideua*, mentioned earlier) not to mention the vegetable dishes (*berenjenas, coles* and *espinacas a la catalana*) some of the most famous being *habas a la catalana* with bacon fat, *butifarra* and

numerous aromatic herbs. Salads too are so versatile that they can be eaten as side dishes, a light main course or even, if a sufficent amount is served attractively, as a first course. Supreme among dessert dishes is the renowned *crema catalana*, followed by the delicate flavour of the *menjar blanc*, the simple and wholesome *mel i mató, postre de músic* and other delicacies. Old and new live side by side in Catalan cookery. Since the beginning of the 20th century Barcelona has been

home to some of the most famous restaurants in Europe and the visitor will find cuisine ranging from Catalan to Spanish regional, from Mediterranean to European and international.

Various types of bars and restaurants exist in Barcelona. The *tasca* is not unlike a tavern; the *bodega* serves draught beer and house wine; a *cafeteria* is like a bar or café; the *cocteleria* is for an aperitif. And then there is the *tapas ritual* – every evening at the bar from 7 to 9 you will find a vast selection of different savouries and nibbles – a delicious choice of flavours, foods and ingredients providing a colourful sight – a feast indeed for the eye and palate!

TAPAS AND STARTERS

In Barcelona's famous tapas bars you will find tasty salads, irresistable prawns, crisp pizzas, as well as the renowned patatas bravas – all delicious savouries to nibble that will stimulate the appetite while chatting.

AMANIDA
Catalonian salad

Young endive, fresh onion, crisp celery – add ham, anchovies, hard-boiled egg, and especially *butifarra*, a local Catalan sausage. This salad can also be a main course accompanied by another speciality – *allioli* – tasty garlic maionnaise.

GAMBAS EN SALSA ROMESCO
Prawns in a spicy sauce dip

Dried sweet peppers, almonds, hazelnuts, garlic, *pimentón fuerte* (hot chile powder), bread crumbs. Combine all in a blender with olive oil and vinegar and you have the perfect salsa *romesco* – ideal for eating with seafood, shellfood, red or white meat, vegetables...

PATATAS BRAVAS
Potatoes in spicy sauce

Cut the potatoes into dice and fry in olive oil. Make a sauce of chopped onions, fried in oil with garlic, dried red chili, chopped ripe tomatoes, and flavoured with a good dry white wine. Toss the fried diced potatoes in the sauce and add some lemon juice.

CIGALAS AL AJO
Garlic scampi

Simple but tasty: scampi, fresh chili peppers, plenty of garlic. Toss all together in a pan with olive oil and salt and pepper.

RICE, PASTA AND SOUPS

Pasta and rice with fish and seafood, or with meat, vegetables, salame, filling and flavoursome cannelloni, tasty soups – each recipe is better than the last. These are really main courses and can be accompanied by a salad.

ARROS AMB CROSTA
Golden rice

A meal in itself based on rice cooked in stock with saffron, *butifarra* (local sausage) – red and white meats, including pork – tomatoes and chick peas. Pour over beaten eggs and cook in oven.

FIDEUA
Pasta paella with fish

An unusual paella in which the rice is replaced by fideos (spaghetti or vermicelli) cooked in stock in a typical Spanish paella dish with onion, garlic, tomatoes, hot chili powder, saffron, parsley and lastly scampi and fish.

CANELONES A LA CATALANA
Catalan-style cannelloni

Exquisite cannelloni filled with pork and chicken. A fluffy beschiamelle sauce, tomato slices, diced ham and the local mahon or manchego cheese grated on top complete the dish, which is cooked in the oven.

SOPA DE MEJILLONES
Mussel soup

Using the most simple of ingredients – onion, garlic, parsley, tomatoes, toasted bread and mussels – this soup belongs to centuries of Spanish traditional cooking. The flavour of this soup is highlighted by a pinch of cinnamon and drop of aniseed liqueur.

149

MEAT AND POULTRY

Lobster and chicken, mussels and pork, snails and rabbit are suitable prime ingredients for traditional recipes from escudella i carn d'olla - soup, main course and side dish all in one - to the magnificent pavo a la catalana or the irresistable paella, here in an excellent local version.

ASADO DE CERDO A LA CATALANA
Roast loin of pork

Herbs – bay leaf, marjoram, parsley and thyme – and spices like cloves, and cinnamon, with onion, garlic and celery give a wonderful flavour to the pork loin, cooked in the oven with a good glass of wine.

PAELLA PARELLADA
Catalan-style paella

This is the most characterisitc Spanish dish, invented in Valencia and famous throughout the world. Based on rice, pork, chicken, seafood, vegetables, garlic, chili peppers and saffron, the Catalonian version includes other ingredients such as mushrooms and / or salame that turn it into a true gastronomic masterpiece.

PAVO A LA CATALANA
Stuffed turkey

A heavy and complex dish that is usually eaten at Christmas. The stuffing includes pork sausage meat and salame, fried in fat with onion, celery, apple, chestnuts, apricots, prunes, sultanas, pinenuts, breadcrumbs and a pinch of cinnamon. Covered with slices of bacon, the turkey is cooked in the oven, occasionally basted with some good Catalan wine.

MAR I TERRA
Chicken with lobster and chocolate

A famous dish that is a synthesis of all Catalan gastronomic expertise. Chicken and lobster are combined in this recipe: the chicken is cooked in fat with onions, leeks, tomatoes, cinnamon and wine, while the lobster is cooked in olive oil. These are then combined in a pastry made of almonds, hazelnuts, garlic, chicken livers and chocolate all chopped up together.

PORC AMB MUSCLOS
Pork and mussels

Cook the pork in a frying pan together with tomatoes, sweet paprika, bay leaf, lemon peel, and chili powder. When almost ready, add the mussels and the water they were cooked in.

ESCUDELLA I CARN D'OLLA
Meats boiled in stock with rice

The Catalan version of the Spanish *cocido*. Veal, chicken, bacon, a pig's ear, cheek and trotter are boiled in stock, and rice or soup pasta are added with saffron. A *pilota*, a large rissole made of pork, fat, egg, garlic, breadcrumbs and parsley is placed in the centre and the dish is served with potatoes, chick peas, carrots, cabbage, celery and turnip.

CONEJO AL ESTILO TARRACONENSE
Casseroled rabbit with chocolate

Flavoured with onion, tomatoes, red wine, fennel seed, nutmeg and a bunch of herbs, the rabbit is cooked with the potatoes and a mixture made of rabbit liver, saffron, chili powder, garlic, plain chocolate and toasted flour.

POLLO EN SAMFAINA
Chicken with aubergine and peppers

Samfaina is a typical Catalan sauce based on aubergines and peppers, with the occasional addition of a courgette, that is perfect with chicken meat, fried in fat with onion, garlic and tomatoes, a glass of white wine and flavoured with bayleaf, parsley and thyme.

ESTOFAT DE BOU
Beef with chocolate

The beef is fried in olive oil while plenty of garlic, onions, carrots, and bacon are cooked in fat and then added to the meat with a handful of herbs, red wine and a tomato. As the sauce is thickening, the grated plain chocolate is added. Delicious with chips.

FISH, SHELLFISH AND SEAFOOD

Both simple and more sophisticated recipes, such as suquet, bring out the exquisite flavours of fresh fish, shellfish and lobsters from the Costa Brava. And not forgetting our earth-bound molluscs, Catalonian cuisine also has many different ways of cooking snails.

CAP ROIG CON SALSA DE AJO
Scorpion fish with garlic

Clean and wash the fish, rub salt over and bake in the oven with olive oil, stock and white wine. Serve with a sauce made with garlic, olive oil and parsley.

DORADA A LA SAL
Orata in salt

This traditional old way of cooking ensures that the fish remains tasty, firm and sweet. The fish is placed on a bed of sea salt, covered with another layer of salt and cooked in the oven. Exquisite with garlic mayonnaise – the local version of aïoli.

JIBIAS CON SETAS
Cuttlefish with mushrooms

The fish are cooked in a sauce of chiles, pepper, tomatoes and onion. Add to this a paste made from garlic, mashed with white wine, and add good quality mushrooms.

PATACO
Tuna with shellfish and vegetables

Cook fresh tuna and clams with onions, tomatoes, potatoes and courgettes in a generous quantity of red wine. Bind the ingredients with *picada* – a typical Catalan sauce of almonds, garlic, parsley, saffron and sweet paprika.

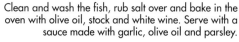

CARACOLES EN LA LLAUNA
Snails gratinée

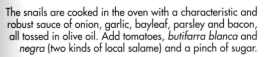

The snails are cooked in the oven with a characteristic and robust sauce of onion, garlic, bayleaf, parsley and bacon, all tossed in olive oil. Add tomatoes, *butifarra blanca* and *negra* (two kinds of local salame) and a pinch of sugar.

SUQUET DE PESCADO CON ALLIOLI
Mixed fish casserole with aïoli

Angler fish, conger eel, cod, prawns, etc. are all cooked with the basic ingredients (onion, tomatoes, garlic, white wine) and combined with two magnificent Catalan sauces: *picada*, an almond-based sauce, and aïoli – garlic mayonnaise found also in Provence.

MEJILLONES RELLENOS
Stuffed mussels

A light summer dish this can also be served as a tasty starter. The mussels are filled with the sauce they are cooked in – onions, garlic, peppers, parsley and a drop or two of wine. Wash down with a glass of excellent white Catalan wine.

LANGOSTA A LA COSTA BRAVA
Lobster with chocolate *picada*

Picada is a spicy base, much used also as a sauce in Catalan cookery. The ingredients can vary occasionally, but almonds are always essential. In this recipe, when the lobster is almost cooked, plain chocolate is added to it and the *picada*.

RAPE EN SALSA DE ALMENDRAS
Angler fish in almond sauce

This delicious fish is fried in olive oil and cooked in the oven with a tasty almond-based sauce of bread crumbs, garlic, chopped parsley and saffron, all bound together with white wine.

EGGS AND VEGETABLES

When accompanied by aïoli, samfaina and sofrito even the vegetable dishes, such as the famous escalivada, in Catalonia become more like main courses than accompaniments.

BERENJENAS A LA CATALANA
Aubergines with nut sauce

The aubergines are fried in olive oil with garlic, onion, tomatoes and then cooked in vegetable stock. Add fried walnuts crushed in a mortar and garnish with chopped parsley.

COLES A LA CATALANA
Cabbage in spicy sauce

A parboiled cabbage cut into strips and cooked in a romesco sauce made of dried sweet peppers, almonds, nuts, garlic, hot chili powder, breadcrumbs, all minced together and combined with olive oil and vinegar. Ideal with pork dishes.

FAVES AL TOMBET
Beans with lettuce

Put broad beans - or haricot beans - in olive oil with sliced lettuce. Make a paste from breadcrumbs lightly fried in olive oil with garlic, minced together and flavoured with vinegar and chili pepper and combine this with the beans and lettuce. Use a vegetable stock to finish the cooking.

PANADONS AMB ESPINACS
Spinach parcels

Toss spinach in a pan with garlic, pine nuts and raisins and then mince together well. Make pastry with flour, water, olive oil and salt; cut into circles and place small amounts of the spinach in the centre. Fold the circles in half to close, brush with beaten egg and bake in the oven.

ESCALIVADA
Oven-baked vegetable salad

An excellent way to appreciate the full flavour of onions, aubergines, tomatoes, peppers. Cook each type of vegetable separately wrapped in tin foil in the oven, then cut into strips and serve dressed with oil etc. as a salad.

PATATAS A LA CERDEÑA
Potatoes with bacon

Delicious potatoes prepared in the simplest way. Boiled and pureed, season with salt and pepper and add bacon fried in olive oil with garlic. Excellent served with red meat.

TORTILLA DE TOMATES Y PIMIENTOS
Tomato and pepper omelette

Tomatoes, peppers and if liked, an aubergine, cut into strips and fried lightly in olive oil. Pour in beaten eggs seasoned with salt and cook the tortilla on both sides.

HABAS A LA CATALANA
Beans with bacon and salame

This vegetable dish is as filling as any main course. Fry bacon in fat with onion and garlic. Add beans and *butifarra blanca* and *negra*, the local Catalan sausage. Cook in plenty of water and add aniseed, cinnamon, herbs and white wine.

TORTILLA DE PATATAS
Potato omelette

A simple recipe with a delicious and unique flavour, this traditional Spanish recipe is especially popular in Catalonia. Cut the potatoes into slices and fry in a pan with some chopped onion. Pour over the beaten eggs seasoned with salt and cook the omelette on both sides.

SWEETS AND DESSERTS

End the meal with a light delicate dessert that recalls forgotten flavours – such as menjar blanc (blancmange) – or old-style family puddings such as the famous Catalan cream.

MENJAR BLANC
Almond puddings

A traditional old Catalan dessert, with a delicate aroma based on almond milk, flavoured with cinnamon, lemon peel and sugar. The ingredients are thickened with cornflour.

CREMA CATALANA
Catalan cream

Made from eggs, milk, sugar, cinnamon and lemon juice, the crema catalana is similar to *tigelada*, a famous Portugese dish. This version is served cold, with brown sugar sprinkled on top and then caramelized.

ENSAIMADAS
Pastry rolls

A speciality from the Balearic islands, now found throughout Spain, these simple and genuine pastry sweets are an example of good, old-fashioned home cooking. Usually eaten at breakfast or coffee time.

GRANIZADO
Lemon granita

With so many citrus fruits produced in the region of Catalonia it is no surprise to find a fresh, thirst-quenching granita of juicy lemons offered as the perfect refresher in the summer heat.

CAVA AND OTHER WINES FROM CATALONIA

At the end of a meal to accompany dessert or to celebrate birthdays and special occasions, there is nothing better than sipping a delicious glass of *Cava*, a spumante produced in this region and exported and appreciated throughout the world. Its excellent quality and reasonable price make it a competitive alternative to French champagne. *Cava* – which literally means 'cellar' – is produced from three local grapes, *Macabeo*, *Xarel-lo* and *Parellada* using the *méthode champenoise*. The best quality Catalan spumante is the *brut de brut* and the *brut nature* followed by *brut* and *sec* which are not quite so dry. The *dulce* and *semiseco* are suitable as

dessert wines. The *Cava rosa*, made by adding some *Pinot Negro*, is also very pleasant. *Cava* comes from a lengthy tradition of wine-making that began in Sant Sadurní d'Ànoia. In 1872 Josep Raventós, the owner of the Codorniu winery, launched a new spumante on the market that was quickly recognised for its high quality, winning a gold medal in 1888. The prestige of the name is still recognised today. The Raventós family has also produced one of the very best *Cava* wines, made in Costers del Segre with the addition of the Chardonnay grape.

157

Just as famous for its high quality is Freixenet, produced in its characteristic black bottle since 1914 by the Sala family of Sant Sadurní d'Anoia. Other types of *Cava* worth mentioning are Gramona, also produced in Sant Sadurní d'Anoia, Mascaró from Vilafranca del Penedès and Raventós Rosell from Masquefa. A visit to the historic *Cava* cellars that are open to the public is very interesting.

Other types of fine wine are produced in Catalonia in the areas of Ampurdán, Alella, Penedès, Priorat and Costers del Segre. So used are people to drinking the nectar of Bacchus in this region that, instead of drinking it from an ordinary glass, it may be poured down the throat from a *porrón*, shaped like a watering can with a long spout from which the liquid merrily flows straight into the throat of the skilled drinker. Since time immemorial, some of the most famous wines have come from Priorat, the area behind Tarragona with a stoney, very flinty earth, where vines were introduced by the Romans and continued to be cultivated on terraces, both natural and manmade, by the monks of the many monasteries in this area. Thanks to the balmy and temperate climate robust wines of 14 to 20 degrees are produced with a characteristic earthy tang. As well as some of the best reds in the world, there are also the straw-coloured white wines with an intense fruity aroma reminiscent of mountain herbs, the rosé and dessert wines. Slightly further to the north are the wines from Penedès, between Tarragona and Barcelona, from vines caressed by marine breezes that rise towards the mighty rampart of Montserrat.

Here too, thanks to the Romans and Benedictine and Cistercian monks, wine has been produced for centuries. These are mainly crisp, fresh young white wines, though today robust red wines are also produced, often matured in barriques, and a suitable accompaniment for the high-class cuisine enjoyed in Catalonia.

INDEX